CREDIT
BUREAUS
SUCK!

By

MICHAEL CITRON

Credit Bureaus Suck!
Copyright © 2011 Michael Citron
All rights reserved

Contents

Introduction

Most companies are in business to sell you something—a new car, fashionable clothing, delicious pizza, or the latest cell phone. You pay the purchase price and in exchange you receive value. If you like the product, you keep it. If you think you got the short end of the stick, you can demand your money back. It's not a perfect system but it works.

How would you feel if you knew that there are major corporations that make huge profits from your misfortunes? Companies that secretly collect information about you and then sell it? Companies that sell *erroneous* information about you and your family, and when it's discovered to be wrong, *you* have to pay to have it corrected, even though the information didn't come from you? And that this bad information can make it impossible for you to buy a house or get a loan?

Such companies exist and, like it or not, they are part of your life.

These companies are consumer credit reporting agencies. You've heard of the Big Three: Experian, TransUnion, and Equifax. These are the companies that collect and sell information about your credit history. These are the companies that assign you—whether you like it or not—a "credit score." It is this credit score, and your full credit report, that can either open doors for you or make your life a living hell.

For most Americans, their credit report is a mystery. Although many of us know our credit score, the system behind that number might as well be a particle accelerator or a nuclear bomb.

As you're about to find out, though, this "mystery" was deliberately created every step of the way. In fact, even the actual formula behind that credit score is a corporate secret—or as their lawyers put it, a "proprietary algorithm." That's the least of it, too. The credit reporting agencies operate in secrecy for a very simple reason: what they do is very clearly an unethical abuse of power.

The system that I will expose here will probably outrage you. This is an industry with no incentive to change because at every turn they are allowed to profit from their own mistakes. Not only does this material make people angry, it's often overwhelming, too. When I present this material live, people begin laughing at the sheer craziness of it all, as I keep laying the unbelievable truth of what these agencies are allowed to do.

This book will go into detail and walk you through the entire industry. And then I'll show you how you can take charge of your credit information, and how you can take on the Goliaths of the credit industry—and win.

Mike Citron

Chapter 1: Credit Makes the World Go Round

Without the ability to get credit, you are essentially a non-citizen. Even if you earn a great living, a history of *paying in cash* is functionally the same as a history of *horrible credit*. Responsible adults without a credit history are forced to start from scratch. These people have to sign up for credit cards and use them so they can demonstrate their ability to make payments as agreed upon. Therefore, it would follow then that living within your means, and paying cash for your purchases, has less value than purchasing items on credit. Logically, it makes no sense. However, it does not need to make sense to consumers; they cannot even challenge the merits of the current credit system. If anything, consumers feel lucky if they are fortunate enough to be extended credit.

This thinking ultimately led to the credit bureaus making the rules that the consumer industry operates under. Who exactly is making the rules and calling the shots? The three major credit bureaus, that's who! The information contained in this book is based on actual accounts from industry insiders, court records, government reports, and recognized authorities.

First, though, let's examine how things came to be this way. How were private corporations allowed to gain such total control over the economic lives of the American people? How can they continue to operate a system that creates damaging errors at random? More importantly, why is it they receive so much support from federal regulators, instead of active investigations and intervention?

History of the Credit Bureaus

In the beginning, the credit bureaus operated in secrecy, using covert methods to gather information from unsuspecting victims. The credit system we know today has evolved from an antiquated manual system, where employees determined consumers' credit worthiness using a subjective system that was unregulated, to one that is almost 100% automated and lacking any semblance of logic, consistency, and fairness for the consumer.

In their early days, the credit bureaus were local, not national. Department stores and other personal finance companies, seeking to share information on their customers, initially established small, localized credit bureaus to service their respective regions. The consumer would apply for credit, and a request was made to the local credit bureau for a recommendation. The credit bureau would in turn, locate the customer's paper file and determine if he or she was a good credit risk and should be extended credit. There was no rating system or set criteria in place which provided a guideline for making such a recommendation.

Unlike today, the consumer had no rights to view their credit file. If somehow the consumer caught wind of an error that existed in their credit file, there were no consumer protections in place to dispute erroneous information.

During that time, credit bureaus would collect every bit of information they could about a person, including employment history, marital status, age, race, religion, testimonials, and any other information they could get their hands on.

With all that information at their fingertips, discrimination was not uncommon. For example, if you lived in the wrong neighborhood or were a part of a minority group that the lender had a personal bias against, you were unable to obtain credit. This infamous practice was known as "red-lining," and it's a tragic case of racist bias that held back the American economy for decades. In fact, today many economists believe that this institutional discrimination actually created a number of small recessions and real estate market crises in most major US cities.

The Welcome Wagon

Over a century ago, members of a group called the Welcome Wagon would personally welcome new neighbors to the neighborhood. Two to three women would prepare some baked goods and personally pay the new neighbor a visit at their home. The visit appeared to be an altruistic overture, but that was not the case. Upon arrival, the women would collect information on the unsuspecting homeowner. They would visually inspect the home, noting the furniture, decorations, fine china, number of children, and anything else that would help them assess the quality of the newcomer.

These women were not reporting the information to the rest of the neighborhood at the weekly neighborhood tea party. The Welcome Wagon actually partnered with the credit bureaus to obtain and share the data—the women were actually employees of the local credit bureaus. At the time, it was the only way the local bureaus could gather information.

The Industry's First Steps Toward Reporting Consistency

Realizing the value of information sharing, in 1906 the credit bureaus established a trade association called the Associated Credit Bureaus (ACB). The ACB's purpose was to facilitate the goals of each bureau and create synergies among the local credit bureaus across the country. The membership quickly grew, but ACB did little more than lay the foundation for the current monopoly on the consumer credit industry by the Big Three consumer credit reporting bureaus that exist today—Experian, Equifax, and TransUnion. (Note: Commercial credit agencies like D&B are different and are not a subject of this book.)

By 1960, the ACB's members had expanded across the country. Due to the fact that computers were not yet available and the information was still in hard copies, credit bureaus covered only a few cities at best. It was during this time that credit cards began to gain popularity. The piecemeal credit review systems in place caused the credit card companies and other lenders to make poor lending decisions, which ultimately led to lost revenues from un-creditworthy consumers who had been extended credit. Either the system needed to be changed, or the credit bureaus would be out of business.

It was also during this time that the federal government had been receiving an increasing number of complaints citing discrimination for home loans. As the federal government regulated the banking industry, in 1971 they took action and enacted the Fair Credit Reporting Act (FCRA). The FCRA forced the credit reporting agencies to reform the existing system of collecting information and assessing credit worthiness. Over time, the information in consumer reports became more reliable, but they were still light years away from being an accurate reflection of the consumers' ability to manage credit.

FICO

It is no exaggeration to say that Fair, Isaac and Company (now known as FICO) revolutionized the credit reporting industry. FICO developed a solution through risk model scoring that was both impartial and consistent. After years of development, the model was released in the 1980s. It was the first version of the rating system we know today as the FICO score.

For every individual who has a credit history, FICO generates a score between 300 (the lowest and worst) and 850 (the highest and best). The average U.S. FICO score[1] is reportedly around 691, with a concentration of about 50% of scores being between 650 and 799.

The system was embraced by the lending industry and credit reporting companies for two reasons.

First, lenders were under scrutiny from Congress to eliminate the current system that enabled and institutionalized discrimination.

Second, the credit bureaus had lost their credibility and needed to do something to stay in business. While the system was embraced, it was not done because of the benefits it offered the industry. Something had to be done to keep business moving forward without further government regulation. This is the first of many instances where the consumer credit industry made decisions based on what was best for the industry, not the consumer.

With the introduction of FICO in the credit reporting arena, individual credit bureaus could use FICO's algorithms to create a single-number credit score in addition to a narrative credit report. This scoring method allowed for faster underwriting because lenders could simply make their underwriting decision based on a score, rather than having to read and judge a traditional, written credit report. This change in credit review made decisions easier for lenders, but horrible for working Americans.

Consumers are now judged not as individuals but as numbers. In addition, the underwriters no longer need to have the in-depth credit knowledge needed to fully analyze a consumer's *true* risk factor. Minor problems like a $150 collection can now lead to a 100-point drop in a FICO score.

As the FICO score became central to the credit and lending industry, lenders were able to implement strict scoring requirements that left no room for interpretation. Lenders wouldn't want to make any manual adjustments anyway, as the correct adjustments would likely not benefit

---

[1] Source: FINRA Investor Education Foundation

them. The deflated credit score based on these small errors allows the lender to impose higher rates and fees on the consumer, which increases their bottom line.

The practice of making credit/underwriting decisions based on a score, rather than full review of a credit history, is harmful to both consumers and lenders. Ultimately the consumer is hurt because they are often less of a risk than the FICO score actually indicates, and therefore their cost of credit should be far less. As recent history proves, with the mortgage and economic debacle it is clear that if a full credit review was used, losses could have been significantly minimized.

The insanity of this tunnel-vision approach becomes clear when you think about real-world examples. It is not uncommon for a 17- or 18-year-old with one credit card and no prior history to have a high credit score. This is exactly why serious economists had been warning for decades that FICO was terrible at really measuring the risk of default—something that should surely be at the core of any credit calculations!

Credit scores *do not* take into account current level of income. Therefore, based on lending practices of the past, a person without employment could qualify for millions in credit simply based on a score calculated by a computer. If lenders were forced to analyze complete credit reports, in addition to the FICO score, the consumer would be charged rates and fees representative of their credit worthiness. Instead, a $150 collection account can cost thousands of dollars in additional interest during the years that it exists on their credit report, regardless of whether or not the company reporting the item can produce documentation to show the validity of the alleged debt.

In recent years, the FICO score has finally come into question. For years, statisticians and academic economists had been publishing studies that indicated the FICO model was actually very weak when it came to predicting the risk of default. Considering we are discussing something called a "credit score," you can see how that's a very big problem.

The real estate crisis that exploded across the US market in 2006 and 2007 made this obscure mathematical argument into headline news around the world. All of a sudden, nobody could ignore the fact that the FICO system, and autopilot computer programs approving loans, were flat-out dangerous for our economy.

That's not the only threat that FICO has been facing. In fact, it turns out that old Fair, Isaac and Company have been basically stabbed in the back by their own customers.

VantageScore

Since the early credit reporting agencies accepted the FICO system by default, it was not a surprise when the VantageScore was first introduced. The VantageScore is a new credit scoring risk model that was developed by the Big Three to compete with the FICO score. How new, you might ask? Well, that's a seriously controversial question that's been argued in federal court. The Vantage score was created to free the credit bureaus from the constraints the FICO score imposed upon them. They wanted to be free from what they perceived as an unfair monopoly that FICO possessed—and as we will soon see, FICO feels quite differently!

The VantageScore is calculated using the same methodology as the FICO score, but adds a few additional metrics in the mix. It assigns a letter grade to your score as well. While FICO scores range from 300 to 850, VantageScores range from 510 to 990. For each 100-point spread on the VantageScore, a letter grade is assigned. For example, 900-990 scores an A. The reporting metrics are similar, but when compared the weighted items in the Vantage report will significantly change the consumer's score, all things being equal.

FICO Score Metrics		VantageScore Metrics	
35%	Payment history	32%	Payment history
30%	Outstanding balances	23%	Amount of credit you're currently using
10%	Types of credit you hold (loans, credit cards, etc.)	15%	Credit balances
15%	Credit history length	13%	Length and depth of credit history (kinds of credit and age of accounts)
10%	Recent history	10%	New credit accounts and inquiries
		7%	Total available credit
100%		100%	

VantageScores are not yet widely used, but lenders are comparing VantageScore to the FICO to determine which is the better option. The lender will disclose the scoring system they are using if you ask. Experian no longer offers the FICO score to the public; they only make the VantageScores available to the public, while TransUnion and Equifax make both available. It appears as if Experian acted as the sacrificial lamb in 2009 by stopping all sales of FICO scores to consumers. They have been the first to stop, in what is believed to be an effort to set the stage, and bring VantageScore to the forefront. Due to the complexities in changing systems and underwriting patterns, lenders have not yet adopted Vantage as an acceptable scoring model. In general, bankers are reluctant to change so it is expected that the VantageScore will not catch on quickly, but based on industry gossip, it appears that a large number of banks are starting to use Vantage scoring simultaneously with FICO scoring, just to start measuring the results. It will take time for lenders to decide which one is a better predictor of risk but when they do, you're likely to see the demise of one of the options.

FICO has responded to Vantage's efforts to dismantle the monopoly by filing massive lawsuits against all three credit reporting bureaus for intellectual property violations. The premise of the suits is that the credit bureaus abused their access to FICO's algorithms to develop the Vantage scoring algorithms. With any high-level corporate lawsuit, however, it may be years before these intellectual property disputes get settled. If and when that finally happens, the effects of that ruling will probably reshape the industry.

Chapter 2: The Big Three Credit Bureaus

It's often assumed that the credit reporting companies are impartial and non-profit, so the actual facts may surprise you. Many Americans even assume that the bureaus are government agencies. This could not be further from the truth.

They may have had humble beginnings, but today, all three consumer credit bureaus have a global presence. Here's a quick look at exactly who we're talking about when we discuss the Big Three.

1. Experian. The Experian Group employs approximately 15,000 people in 40 countries, supporting clients in more than 65 countries around the world. Total Group revenue for the year ending March 31, 2012 was $4.5 billion. Although they control the economic fates of millions of American citizens, they're not even a US company. Their headquarters is in Dublin, Ireland and their main offices are in Nottingham, England. Experian was created during a flurry of buyouts and consolidation, getting most of their data from the purchase of TRW Information Services, a 100-year-old credit agency and one of the oldest such firms in America. Since then, they've expanded in very telling directions, purchasing email marketing companies, data-mining and surveillance startups, and several debt consolidation and collection firms. Clearly, they're seeing a much bigger future than just credit reports.

2. Equifax. It seems like Equifax has always been in the business—they were founded way back in 1899. Their annual revenues in 2011 were $1.96 billion and they operate in fourteen countries, although, like TransUnion, they are based in the US. Equifax is also the largest of the Big Three. From their headquarters in Atlanta, Georgia, they manage the undisputed heavyweight champion of databases: an astronomical 400 million individual files. That's bigger than the entire population of the United States!

Not only that, but Equifax has been causing controversy for almost as long as they've been in business. During the 1960s and 70s, Equifax was repeatedly rocked by scandals when it was revealed they ran a cash incentive program to reward employees for uncovering negative information about consumers. As you can see, this predatory pattern is actually nothing new. It's disturbing to see how long Equifax has been playing the same dirty game.

3. TransUnion. Unlike the other two Big Three firms, TransUnion is privately held so they don't have to declare much in the way of earnings or corporate information. They got their start in the personal information business when they bought out the Cook County Credit Bureau, one of the original Welcome Wagon firms we were discussing at the beginning of this report. In other words, they bought the financial history of the entire city of Chicago in one purchase! Since then, they focused on acquiring more lists from around the world, although they still call Chicago home.

TransUnion was party to a notable and precedent-setting case for the credit repair industry. A courageous and very patient woman by the name of Judy Thomas successfully sued TransUnion for a whopping $5.3 million dollars. Her story was particularly outrageous. She uncovered a simple, glaring error in her credit report and took all the legal steps to get it amended. The process wound up costing her endless hours of paperwork and no less than *six years* to finally get the false information removed from her credit report.

All three agencies have something else in common: In 2000, they were all fined by the Federal Trade Commission for willfully violating the Fair Credit Reporting Act. The FTC concluded they were deliberately blocking and delaying phone calls and correspondence from consumers who were trying to get information about their credit.

These were not even people trying to dispute errors—these were Americans trying to exercise their simple legal rights to access their own information! The total amount of the settlement was a slap on the wrist: $2.5 million dollars. Split between The Big Three, of course, that amounts to almost nothing. They didn't reconsider their deceptive practices; they just kept on doing what they do best. Which brings us the ugliest chapter of all: just what, exactly, are these all-powerful corporations doing with your records?

Chapter 3: How the Credit Bureaus Make Money

You may be wondering about a common-sense question at this point: what's the business model? What stake do these consumer credit bureaus have in the consumer credit industry?

In simpler times, the three credit bureaus made money honorably—they charged a fee for credit reports and credit scores. As technology became more sophisticated and the credit bureaus experienced an increase in their power over the financial industry, things changed. They quickly realized that information is power and leveraged that power into profits.

Soon, other businesses began popping up that made money off related consumer services such as credit repair, credit monitoring, and debt reduction. This is when the consumer began to really get the short end of the stick while everyone else made money. One would think that the companies selling services to repair credit, resolve ID theft, and monitor credit reports would be a great benefit to the consumer, but actually the consumer is a pawn in the credit game. As the companies attempt to help consumers repair their credit and resolve ID theft, they typically act with great integrity and intentions, but you will soon learn the biggest obstacle that these companies face is the credit bureaus. You would think that the bureaus would help these companies to help consumers but the truth is far from that. To further their monopoly and continue to profit from their own errors and inadequacies, they actually try to block, and even put out of business, all of these consumer advocate companies.

These private corporations have been allowed to make mistakes that have a tremendous effect on our lives. Rather than be held accountable, they have been allowed to monetize every error they make. Anyone can see this is a dangerous recipe for corruption—and without question, that's precisely what has come to pass. The behavior and business practices of the Big Three are beyond irresponsible.

Sometimes it can be hard to get perspective on something we deal with every day, and the concept of credit is no exception. The whole purpose of this book is to make this invisible world less mysterious, so let's pause for a moment and consider a hypothetical situation—a "thought experiment" to illustrate how absurd our credit reporting really is.

A 5,000-Foot View

Consider an example of a person who pays cash for everything. The time comes when he or she wants to buy a home. Now, they need to establish a credit history, as the average person cannot pay cash for a home. Their history of saving for their purchases and living within their financial means cannot be quantified. He or she can produce bank statements and years of utility bills, insurance bills and other statements showing that they have paid their bills on time, but they don't count. Despite the fact that they have been financially responsible for their entire life, they still need a credit history that is accepted by the financial community—a FICO score. This is an artificial need imposed by the credit bureaus, who insist that you are nothing without a FICO score or credit history that is tracked in their database.

The consumer is forced to open up credit accounts in order to get on the credit bureaus' radar and establish enough of a payment history to produce a FICO score. Because our thrifty cash-paying friend has no established credit, the only credit accounts they will be eligible for will charge them a high interest rate. And because they must show that they can carry a balance over time and pay responsibly, they cannot avoid this high rate by paying off the credit card balance each month. (Keep in mind that each of the accounts to which the consumer will apply in order to establish credit will purchase a copy of the consumer's report from at least one of the Big Three. Hmm, sounds like they're saying "cha-ching" every time they apply.)

Once the consumer establishes a credit history, he or she can apply for a home loan. The consumer is charged a loan application fee, part of which is paid to the three credit bureaus to obtain his FICO score and credit reports. Isn't that nice? This is only one of several methods that the credit bureaus will make money off of this one consumer over his or her lifetime. When—inevitably—a creditor inaccurately reports information on his or her credit report, the credit bureaus have even found a way to make money on that! When the victim's identity is stolen, they will cash in yet again.

However, I am getting ahead of myself. To see how credit bureaus make money from your misfortune, let's start from the very beginning.

Data Sales

The first way the credit bureaus make money is from selling the data they collect. Instead of the Welcome Wagon collecting the information, data now comes from a variety of sources: collection agencies, credit card companies, banks, student loan providers, utility companies, finance companies, and *you*. That's right: every time you fill out a loan application, all of the data on that application gets transmitted to the credit bureaus—your address, work history, how many children you have, your income—everything. Additionally, credit bureaus purchase data from other credit bureaus. For example the Big Three credit bureaus will often contract with third-party information providers like Lexis Nexis, who often provide them with public record data. By having third parties provide reporting data, credit bureaus must rely on the accuracy of that data, and often cannot prove the accuracy, timeliness and verifiability of the data provided to them. This in turn, could severely infract the FCRA by violating the three basic principles of all items that are reporting on your credit report, which are:

1) Be reporting within the legal allowable reporting period of 7, 10, or 15 years; *and*

2) Be reporting 100% accurate information; *and*

3) Be reporting 100% *verifiable* information.

When consumers apply for credit, they provide the credit reporting agencies with data. When you and I secure credit, we continue to provide data based on payment habits and the way we manage our credit lines. Unlike the 1960s, where a human was required to manually update hard copy credit files, technology has enabled the collecting data to become an automated, passive process. When a lender summits a request for a consumer credit report, the reporting agency forwards the information electronically.

Additionally, regular updates from all subscribers are required to be sent to all three credit bureaus monthly via electronic means such as the Metro 2 reporting format. The process has been systemized so no human actually has to have any interaction. It practically runs itself.

What I'm about to discuss here is the hidden market for information about you—your life, your money, your relationships, and your private records. This is a massive source of easy profits, and this is something that every credit reporting bureau would prefer that the American public absolutely never learns about because they know the outrage it would provoke.

Not only is your data not safe in their hands, it's even got a price tag attached. The credit reporting agencies sell two types of data: consumer credit report data and direct marketing data.

Consumer Credit Report Data

Consumer credit report data is used by lenders to evaluate a consumer's credit risk and ability to pay back the debt. Lenders, landlords, employers, credit card companies, insurance companies, and licensing agencies purchase consumer data from the credit reporting agencies. They pay a fee to obtain an electronic copy of applicants' credit histories. When you consider the number of times that you have consented to have your credit report run, the credit bureaus are making a tremendous amount of money selling this data. Each time your credit is pulled by someone attempting to make a credit decision, the inquiry is noted on your credit file. Based on the laws of the FCRA, anyone who obtains a copy of your credit report must be noted on your report. FICO's scoring model considers frequent inquiries as an indication that the consumer is actively seeking credit and possibly *a greater risk*. There is potentially additional risk if any of those credit lines that were applied for had been obtained and are not yet on the report. In addition, consumers who apply for too many lines of credit are not demonstrating good judgment in the eyes of lenders and the FICO scoring model.

The credit-scoring model does not punish consumers for viewing their own report. So consumers can go to any of the online sites to get copies of their report as often as they wish with *no* effect on their credit score.

Direct Marketing Data

The credit bureaus also sell data to marketing companies that want to reach consumers within a certain demographic, with the intention of selling those consumers their products and services. For example, a local Honda dealership wants to use direct mail to reach consumers who would potentially qualify for their 0% financing program. They may need the information on consumers within a fifty-mile range with a credit score of 750 or above. The credit bureaus provide this information to the Honda dealer. These marketing inquiries must also be reflected in a consumer's version of their credit report, but they are not visible to anyone but the consumer, therefore, they do not affect the credit score.

You can take action. I always advise consumers to *opt out* of their information being sold to marketers. This helps in the credit repair and rebuilding process for a variety of reasons, but most importantly, your information is kept private and cannot be sold if you have opted out.

To opt out, go to www.OptOutPrescreen.com. This will stop the credit bureaus from selling your data, which will significantly decrease the amount of junk mail that you get.

Not All Data Is Created Equal

Ready for the next big secret? I'm afraid it gets even worse from here. As you're about to see, not only are the Big Three making a killing selling your personal information, but they've also got an actual financial stake in gathering as many poor credit scores as possible.

Some data is more valuable than other data, which allows the credit bureaus to charge more for it. As sick as it sounds, there is more money to be made in people with problem credit because they can be taken greater advantage of.

Consider a Honda dealership. Margins on selling cars are quite tight, and as a dealer you make your money on upselling, financing, and fees. When you get consumers who are fortunate enough to have high credit scores, they will qualify for the promotional offers, commonly 0% to 5% financing. That's great news for them but nobody in your sales department is very happy about it. The dealership will sell a car, but make less profit on the financing.

Now, here's what keeps car dealerships honest, in theory: they have huge cash incentives to keep vehicles moving off the lot and clear out new-car shipments as quickly as possible. For that reason, getting customers with solid credit is often the best way to move a large quantity of vehicles out and keep profits high. Overhead expenses demand they not take advantage of too many customers.

This is not always the case, though.

Now consider a credit card company that charges outrageous fees and inflated interest rates to high-risk consumers. They want to market to people with *less-than-average credit*. The methodology is that these consumers will be willing to pay more to have a credit card because their credit is poor. People with harmed, bruised, or sub-prime credit are the people who make the banks the most amount of money in fees and interest. The only trick is that the lender doesn't want too many borrowers defaulting.

Finally, consider the sales department at one of the Big Three credit bureaus. Their sole job is maximizing the income they can generate off their data. (Of course, it's actually *your* data, but put yourself inside their heads for a moment.) When it comes to making the most money off a credit report, which client do you think will be willing to pay the most for leads—the Honda dealership or the credit card company?

The problem is that predatory lenders are the best customers that the credit reporting agencies could ask for. This is because they're willing to pay top dollar prices in order to get access to the bottom-of-the-barrel FICO scores. This is a serious problem—and unfortunately it gets even worse.

The Credit Score Sweet Spot

Rock-bottom credit scores, of course, are financial poison, but there exists a sweet spot of marginal credit scores just under the threshold (typically between 540 and 699) where the risk is basically identical but the banks will make out because they can charge higher fees and interest rates. Marginal scores are a gold mine because those consumers can get credit, but inevitably wind up paying far more than they should.

Here's the horrible real-world consequence of all that: now the credit bureaus have no incentive to correct inaccurate data. After all, the worse the credit score, they more money the credit bureaus make on selling it. In addition to selling the bad data, the credit bureaus also make money on the dispute process. If you were the credit bureaus, what would you do? There are numerous examples of cases that were compiled in a 2009 NCLC (National Center for Consumer Law) study entitled *Automated Injustice: How a Mechanized Dispute System Frustrates Consumers Seeking to Fix Errors in Their Credit Reports,* in which it has been uncovered that all three credit bureaus actually profit from credit reporting errors. (More on this report in a minute.)

Chapter 4: David v. Goliath and the Dispute Process

This fact has never been exposed like this. The truth is hidden amongst congressional testimony and buried in back pages of unexposed reports—until now. Based on information from congressional hearings and insider information the truth is now out: the credit bureaus actually make money on the dispute process. Let's pause for a moment and consider that the credit bureaus make the most money selling data about those people with the worst credit histories. These are the same companies who are responsible for the dispute process and correcting your credit file. It is a classic example of hiring the fox to guard the henhouse. Since negative data is more valuable than accurate data, the credit bureaus have no real incentive to maintain accurate data in the system. Once the consumer is compromised, they're in the money. You'd think that the fines or lawsuits levied against these companies for their actions would be motivation to correct their practices, but the truth is far from that.

We've already discussed the outcome of one of the lawsuits against them—a fine of $2.2 million. To these companies, though, that's likely just the cost of doing business, and as long as they can continue to maintain a healthy profit after paying these piddly fines, they'll continue on, as they have for decades.

Under the Fair Credit Reporting Act (FCRA):

1. You have the right to dispute unverifiable, outdated or inaccurate information contained in your credit report.

2. Unless your dispute is obviously frivolous, the credit bureau must investigate all inaccurate information. There is an established process outlined by the FCRA.

3. Once it is identified, the inaccurate, incomplete, or unverifiable information must be removed or corrected within thirty days.

4. Outdated negative information must be removed as well.

While these rights may seem to benefit the consumer, once again we will see that the true beneficiaries in the credit industry are the credit reporting agencies.

Back in the good old days, when disputes were actually done via snail mail and a real live person worked the dispute, it is completely reasonable to believe that the process cost the credit reporting agencies money. With the technology used today, it is a fairly automated process of straight data transfer. Still, no matter how simple the process is, the credit reporting agencies continue to stonewall disputes and complain about what a burden they are.

The credit reporting agencies estimate that more than 30% of the disputes they process are submitted by credit repair companies and the other 70% are submitted by consumers. They also claim that at least 30% of the total dispute claims filed are frivolous and an abuse of the system. They insist that processing these disputes actually costs them money but as it is required under the FCRA, they are legally bound to respond to each and every non-frivolous compliant.

The critical piece of this puzzle is that the paying clients of the credit reporting industry are not *consumers*, but the *creditors* who both furnish and use the information contained in the credit bureaus' databases. For example, discovery in recent lawsuits has uncovered the fact that TransUnion had received over $6 million per year from MBNA (Maryland Bank of North America) alone.

Litigation discovery has also shown that the credit bureaus have made it their business to drive down the cost of disputes to such a low point that processing these disputes has become a substantial source of revenue stream for the credit bureaus. The system blatantly violates the FCRA, but the risk of an occasional FCRA lawsuit doesn't seem to be effecting their procedures.

Do The Math

According to *Automated Injustice*, outsourcing has become a highly profitable business for the credit bureaus. Before 2004, when Equifax still handled some disputes in-house, its average cost per dispute was $4.67. Toward the end of 2004, Equifax began using an outsource vendor called ACS in Montego Bay, Jamaica. ACS investigations cost Equifax only $1.08 each. An almost 80% cost reduction was apparently not enough, though. As it stands today, DDC, an agency in the Philippines, has enabled Equifax to reduce the cost to $0.57 per dispute, despite the number of accounts that are disputed.

Credit reports are so inaccurate that when consumers requested a free copy of their report after suffering a credit denial, 75% thereafter informed the bureaus that the report contained inaccuracies. The average consumer has five errors on their credit report!

So what happens next? The consumer files one dispute to cover all five errors. The credit bureau forwards the dispute to the outsourcing agency overseas and pays them $0.49 to process all five errors. The credit bureaus charge a fee to data furnishers for providing incorrect data. Each dispute on a report is assessed a $0.25 fee per bureau; therefore, if five items are disputed each credit reporting agency charges $1.25 to the lending institution that reported the information incorrectly (five errors @ $0.25 each). The bottom line is a $0.76 profit on a $0.49 investment.

Hooray for Capitalism!

While this information is public record, based on Congressional testimony, it has not been widely reported on any media outlet, including the Internet. Considering the number of people who are injured by the credit bureaus need to turn a profit from everything they do, one would assume that the report would have made national headlines. However, due to the credit reporting agencies considerable investment in propaganda campaigns, advertising and lobbying, negative information about them is rarely publicized.

Chapter 5: Credit Monitoring and ID Theft

When a consumer applies for credit, a company that is authorized to obtain a copy of the consumer's report will electronically submit a request for the report. The request must contain specific data about the consumer in order for the credit bureau to extract the correct report. It is surprising to learn that one of the critical pieces of data, the consumer's Social Security number, is not needed in order to obtain the report or extend credit! Wow! The credit bureaus only require minimal match requirements prior to providing a report to an authorized party.

The credit bureaus' refusal to require an 8/9 or 9/9 match on SSN due to efficiency and profitability concerns leaves the door wide open for ID theft. One would assume that the credit bureaus would view ID theft as a risk to the integrity of their databases and an injury to the consumer that should be avoided. Not so much! Once the credit bureaus realized that identity theft products and related services could be just one more way to make money, they had no incentive to do anything to truly secure consumers' credit data.

All three credit bureaus offer some form of credit monitoring service that lure the consumer into thinking that while they are helpless against ID theft in general, at least they can be notified when someone attempts to steal their good credit. For the credit bureaus, this a huge win as they can finally make money from those who have good credit. As you recall, the data of individuals with poor credit is of significantly more value than those with stellar credit histories.

Perversely enough, failing to take any precautions to hinder ID theft creates an additional source of income for the credit reporting agencies. The bureaus earn millions of dollars per year in credit monitoring services from consumers who are running scared from ID theft. The consumers who do not opt for credit monitoring services will usually pay fees to review their credit reports more frequently. After all, most would think $15 is a small fee to pay to keep your credit and identity safe, right?

Those With Good Credit: The Final Frontier?

The credit reporting agencies have now found a very creative method to turn a profit from those consumers with good credit scores. Traditionally, the market segment of consumers with good credit was not as profitable for credit reporting agencies as those with poor histories. These are the segment of society that historically, applies for less credit, and whose data is less valuable because they demand lower interest and no/low fees.

Additionally, this demographic will statistically have fewer "pulls per purchase." It's actually simple to understand. Those with marginal credit will have their credit reviewed (cha-ching for the bureaus) more often when buying a car, a home, or applying for a credit card. The consumers with marginal scores will be applying more often due to increased denials and unfavorable terms that they are shopping around to try and beat. Those consumers with stellar credit will more often negotiate the best deal immediately, knowing that they will qualify therefore they don't have to shop around, and hence get less pulls per purchase.

Credit Monitoring Is Not a Public Service

By now, it is abundantly clear that the credit reporting agencies primary objective is to turn a profit, generally at the expense of the consumer. Instead of fulfilling their duties under the FCRA, the national CRAs have developed credit-monitoring and related services as a growing and substantial profit center marketed through the threat and fear of identity theft and other similar credit reporting inaccuracies.

Most people have seen the catchy commercials for FreeCreditReport.com. What most people do not know is that FreeCreditReport.com is actually a credit monitoring service *owned by Experian*. In its May 23, 2007 report to shareholders, Experian reported:

"Consumer Direct [online credit reports, scores and monitoring services] delivered excellent growth throughout the period, with strong demand from consumers for credit monitoring services, which led to higher membership rates."

Under the FCRA, the credit reporting agencies have an obligation to provide free credit reports to consumers. After FACTA, consumers are entitled to receive one free report from each CRA per year. If the consumer has been denied credit, is indigent, or suspects possible fraud or identity theft, their additional reports are also free. The annual fee charged at freecreditreport.com charges the consumer for information that they are entitled to for free, under certain circumstances. The service is essentially useless and redundant for the consumer.

Additionally, consumers are entitled to the ultimate credit protection program via Credit Freeze. For a low one-time fee of $5, consumers can *completely* freeze access to their credit reports. Upon submission of a credit freeze request, the consumer is issued a secure PIN that must be released prior to anyone gaining access to their report. This is the ultimate in credit identity protection—and yet, you rarely see information about this advertised anywhere!

Equifax has reported that credit monitoring services account for 10% of their total revenue. On its Internet home page, www.equifax.com, Equifax sells its credit monitoring products to consumers stating, "Make sure your reports are accurate & free of fraud." Isn't credit report accuracy a right under the FCRA? Imagine if a physician advertised a service that "guaranteed" the patient confidentiality regarding their medical records.

Let's say that your bank begins offering a service to customers that provides overdraft protection when you bounce a check as a result of the teller making a clerical error. No reasonable consumer would purchase such a service, as he would hold the bank liable for the error and demand the overdraft fees be reversed. H&R Block offers a similar service to their customers that offers insurance if the tax preparer makes an error on your income tax return. It makes no sense!

If a zoo notified the local residents that they need to be on guard for escaped lions, the public would be outraged that the zoo was not taking the steps necessary to ensure that the lions remained in their cages. Instead of revamping and repairing the system that allows it to exist, the credit reporting agencies have made the public scared to death of ID theft.

The Numbers Tell the True Story

Fraud complaints made up 55% of all the FTC complaints in 2011. Identity theft is the #1 complaint type the FTC receives. Identity theft accounts for 15% of all complaints compared to #2, debt collector complaints (10%), and #3, "Prizes, Sweepstakes and Lotteries" complaints (6%). These numbers are enough to make any citizen take notice. For those with high credit scores, the numbers are alarming. As those with high credit scores tend to take fewer risks, they are likely to purchase credit-monitoring services. The credit monitoring services market is dominated by the three major credit bureaus and is fueled by concerns about the number one ranking complaint: ID theft.

RANK	CATEGORY	COMPLAINTS	PERCENT
1	Identity Theft	279,259	15%
2	Third Party and Creditor Debt Collection	180,928	10%
3	Prizes, Sweepstakes and Lotteries	100,208	6%
4	Shop-at-Home and Catalog Sales	98,306	5%
5	Banks and Lenders	89,341	5%
6	Internet Services	81,805	5%
7	Auto Related Complaints	77,435	4%
8	Impostor Scams	73,281	4%
9	Telephone and Mobile Services	70,024	4%
10	Advance-Fee Loans and Credit Protection/Repair	47,414	3%
11	Foreign Money Offers and Counterfeit Check Scams	43,101	2%
12	Health Care	38,246	2%
13	Mortgage Foreclosure Relief and Debt Management	38,140	2%
14	Credit Cards	37,932	2%
15	Television and Electronic Media	37,404	2%
16	Business Opportunities, Employment Agencies and Work-at-Home Plans	36,111	2%
17	Internet Auction	35,926	2%
18	Travel, Vacations and Timeshare Plans	32,736	2%
19	Credit Bureaus, Information Furnishers and Report Users	30,203	2%

If the numbers are accurate, then ID theft is a serious problem in the United States. But that's not the case. In fact, they are misleading because, as I'll explain below, almost 44% of reported incidents of identity theft are actually credit reporting inaccuracies that are being *reported* as ID theft. So if you extrapolate 44% of the ID theft complaints as reported by the FTC, and reassign them to the true cause, the credit reporting agencies would actually be the #1 industry on the FTC's list of reported complaints, closely followed by identity theft itself. These same inaccuracies continue to be perpetuated by the credit reporting agencies due to their refusal to reform the automated system that exists for credit reporting.

A study of credit scores for mortgage applicants by the Consumer Federation of America and the National Credit Reporting Association found that one in ten files (155 out of 1,545) contained at least one and as many as three additional repository consumer reports, and that it was very common for the additional reports to contain a mixture of credit information, some of which belonged to the subject of the report requested and some which did not.

Common reasons for the additional reports include:

1. Confusion between generations with the same name (Jr., Sr., II, III, etc.).
2. Mixed files with similar names, but different social security numbers.
3. Mixed files with matching social security numbers, but different names.
4. Mixed files that listed accounts recorded under the applicant's name, but with the Social Security number of the co-applicant.
5. Name variations that appeared to contain transposed first and middle names.
6. Files that appeared to track credit under the applicant's nickname.
7. Spelling errors in the name.
8. Transposing digits on the social security number.

The results of the study revealed that almost 44% of the complaints that are reported as ID theft should be classified as a credit bureau complaint. It is mind boggling to think that with the technology available today, these errors and inaccuracies are allowed to exist. It is not the technology but the gross negligence that exists when the data that is matched to individual credit files by the system.

A substantive explanation of the CRA matching process was provided in a 2005 deposition of Equifax's vice president of technology:

Q. And what is required to match a tradeline to an existing file?

A. We use the L90 search logic, which has thirteen matching elements, and based on those thirteen matching elements, we have an internal algorithm that makes the determination whether the ID matches sufficiently to apply the trade.

Q. If a first and last name and the full Social Security number on the tradeline match an existing file, would Equifax report that tradeline to the existing file?

A. Yes, given there was not other information that was in conflict that prevented that, that kind of took away from the positive match of a name and a Social then, yes, I believe it would. I would like to see the specific example, though.

Q. What if the current address is on the existing file and the new tradeline did not match?

A. If the Social Security number matches, that's normally enough information to allow it to update, even if the address does not match.

Chapter 6: Automated Disputes

As they were not already making a ton of money and injuring consumers in the process, the credit bureaus have found another way to defraud the public even more. They created an online system to automate everything they were doing wrong, and had the audacity to present it as an outreach program to help consumers!

The automated dispute system requires that the consumer log onto the dispute site and enter in the information regarding the erroneous items. The customer dispute is then converted to a three-digit code. The code is then forwarded to the reporting agency for investigation.

At first glance, the online disputing system appears to be a benefit to the consumer. The only benefit to the consumer is the ease and convenience of filing an online dispute instead of actually writing a letter to dispute the item. That part is a benefit, but disputing your items online is actually a great disadvantage to the consumer due to the part of the process that appears on the surface to be a benefit. In reality, what it does is strip the consumer's legal rights, while making it easy for the credit bureaus to further their agenda. Let's examine how they do this.

The 30-Day Time Limit - The FCRA imposes a thirty-day time limit on the dispute. If the item is not responded to within that time limit, it must be removed from your credit file. Using the automated dispute system makes it very easy for the credit reporting bureau and reporting agency to not only respond, but to respond without having to do a full investigation.

Paper Trail - Using the automated dispute system does not create a paper trail for the consumer to track the details of the dispute. As a result, the consumer does not have a paper trail if they have to take further legal actions for non-compliance by the credit bureaus. This is not an accident.

Limited Dispute Reasons - Due to the electronic coding system, there is an inherent limitation for disputing. The coding system is limited to the codes that are in existence. There is no place for you to send all relevant information about the dispute to the furnisher of data. Under the FCRA, all relevant information must be transmitted to the data furnisher. The online dispute system circumvents that requirement and sabotages the entire process. The online dispute system has a place for "other information," but the amount of space allowed is barely enough for a couple sentences. How could someone accurately describe a dispute in less than two sentences?

Expeditious Dispute Resolution - The Fair Credit Reporting Act section 611a(8) changes the standard requirements and protections afforded to the consumer by the FCRA when the consumer uses the online dispute process.

The FCRA Expeditious Dispute Resolution section states:

"The agency shall not be required to comply with paragraphs 2, 6, and 7 with respect to that dispute if they delete the trade line within 3 days."

Paragraph 2 requires the credit bureau to forward your dispute and all related documentation you provide to the creditor. The online dispute process does not allow for any paperwork or documentation to be provided, nor considered in the process.

What consumers are not aware of is that if credit bureaus delete an item without forwarding your dispute to the data furnisher, the data furnisher will re-report this item in the next reporting cycle. The data furnisher will most likely not be aware of your dispute therefore they may simply re-insert the item. There is a standard notice that is required to be sent prior to any reinsertion of a deleted item, however based on the law, if you dispute online, the credit reporting agencies *do not* have to follow that part of the law. The credit reporting agencies *do not* have to send you a notice prior to reinsertion if you dispute online. This information that would protect consumers from their federally granted rights being stripped from them has been barely accessible—until now!

Paragraph 6 requires the credit bureau to provide you with written results.

Paragraph 7 requires the credit bureau to provide you with the method of verification on request from the consumer.

"Method of verification" is a powerful tool in the dispute process. If expeditious dispute resolution is used, the right to utilize this tactic is eliminated. So we have to ask: who is this really "expeditious" for?

No Real Investigation

The dispute system was created to provide the consumer recourse when there is an inaccuracy on their credit report. The way the system has turned into an automated dispute process is fundamentally flawed. There are no real investigations, but rather an automated process of sending and receiving information between the financial institution and the credit reporting agencies. The process barely satisfies the FCRA regulations and frequently violates the law.

Now, the *big zig* to online disputing that's hidden beneath the surface. The credit reporting agencies seem to be quite intuitive at finding hidden profit centers. Just when you thought they had all the angles covered the deep truth of online disputing is exposed. When consumers dispute online, there are no interactions with the humans needed to facilitate the dispute process—not even the low-priced, foreign outsourced labor. Online disputes are truly 100% automated by computer systems—and the credit reporting agencies still charge the data furnishers for the errors. With this method, their profit on disputes is nearly 100% —*wow*!

The Use of Automated Systems

The investigations usually involve the furnisher (or creditor) comparing the information in their computers to what is reported in your credit file. Typically the bureau accepts what the furnishing company tells them. This is referred to as "parroting," as the reporting agency is simply repeating what the furnisher has said. There is no additional investigation to review records or contact the consumer.

The automated dispute system is designed to convert the detailed reporting information into a simple three-digit code and a couple of lines of narrative. There is a standard form which all three reporting agencies use for this process called the Consumer Dispute Verification form (CDV). If the form is submitted electronically, it is known as an Automated Consumer Dispute Verification (ACDV) form. The ACDV form consists of a few pieces of information: the consumer's identifying information, the codes which summarize the dispute, and sometimes a couple of lines of narrative.

The credit bureaus' e-OSCAR system (Online Solution for Complete and Accurate Reporting) offers 26 available dispute codes: not his/hers, account closed, account paid as agreed, etc. These codes are what drive the system, yet they are inadequate in many instances to convey a complete picture of the actual dispute.

The investigation is initiated by the credit bureau by sending the CDV through the automated processing system called e-OSCAR. Despite the fact that the consumer has most likely sent in supporting documentation and a detailed description of the dispute, a three-digit code is all that is actually transmitted to the reporting agency. It should be noted that the employees who do the coding are not instructed to do anything but locate the code which best describes the dispute. They are not required, nor encouraged, to read all of the attached documentation or attempt to analyze the situation. What makes matters worse is that there were originally 100 codes, but they were reduced to only 26. Again, this was not done to make life easier for you and me—this is designed to "expedite" corporate profits.

Out of the 26 codes, the credit bureaus actually assign almost 85% of the disputes to only five of the 26 available codes.

CODE	PERCENTAGE
Not his/hers	30.5%
Disputes present/previous account status/history	21.2%
Claims inaccurate information. Did not provide specific dispute	16.8%
Disputes amounts	8.8%
Claims account closed by consumer	7.0%
TOTAL	84.3%

Coding Process Is a Violation of FCRA

As you recall, it was the FCRA that established fair reporting practices and afforded consumers the ability to dispute inaccurate information on their credit report. Within the FCRA is an explicit requirement that the credit bureau include in the notice of dispute to the furnisher all relevant information provided by the consumer. Regardless of the amount of information that the consumer submits with their dispute, the automated dispute system will reduce all of the information that a consumer submits to a three-digit code. The bureau does not forward the supporting documents that the consumer has provided. This documentation can include account applications, billing statements, communications between the consumer and reporting agency, and even conclusive proof of the consumer's dispute.

For years now, consumers have complained about the bureaus' refusal to include the supporting evidence with the dispute. Attorneys have taken note and are claiming that this refusal is a clear violation of the FCRA.

The credit bureaus assert that forwarding documents through e-OSCAR is "questionable." This is doubtful, as the electronic transmission of documents is easy to say the least. Anyone who has successfully attached a file to an email can verify this for themselves. Since all three credit bureaus already scan and archive the consumer's dispute documents, we know that they have the capability to do it. They already have the storage available and are already paying their employees to do the scan. Equifax and TransUnion are currently sending the supporting documents to India and the Philippines. Sending them through the e-OSCAR system would be downright simple—not "questionable."

The credit bureaus' rebuttal to this claim is that the ACDV form has a free text field that permits the credit bureaus' clerks to offer additional explanation. As this field limits the number of characters that can be entered, the field is simply not sufficient. In addition, the credit bureau employee procedure manuals do not offer guidelines that indicate what information should be included. As a result, the clerks seldom utilize this field. During an FTC hearing, one credit bureau clerk indicated that if he could choose a category that was sufficient for the dispute, he saw no reason to utilize the text field at all!

The Truth of the Matter

The credit bureaus' employees are crippled by systems that are designed for profit, not for accuracy. These systems do not have the ability to transmit documents to the data furnisher, nor is any true investigation supported by the credit reporting agencies. The end result is a one-sided verification of the data that they have in the system, without any consideration for the additional data provided by the consumer.

Essentially, the investigations are limited to *categorizing* disputes. This is supported by the internal handbooks of the credit bureaus and evidence in FCRA lawsuits. The result is that the primary job of these employees, or in most cases outsourced vendors, is no more than selecting the appropriate dispute codes to send to the furnisher. As there is no discretion on the part of the employee, there clearly is no investigation.

TransUnion procedures were further elaborated upon in this deposition of an employee who performed dispute processing—that is, before her job was outsourced to a vendor in India:

Q. [If the] consumer says, "Dispute this credit card account, here's the account number, it belongs to my husband, not to me, what would you have done if you were complying with TransUnion procedures in August 5?

A. I would dispute the account with the appropriate claim code.

Q. How would you do that?

A. In the computer. [. . .] I would click on the account and select the appropriate claim code. Once you hit okay, it says open, which means the dispute on that account has been opened.

Q. After you put the dispute code and click on the dispute, do you have any other role in the investigation or dispute process for that account?

A. No.

Q. It just gets sent onto the creditor, and your job as to that dispute is done, right?

A. Correct.

Q. It would be fair to say that if you were complying with TransUnion's policies, you're not as an investigator or as a dispute processor making any judgment calls or exercising any discretion about whether a consumer really owns the account? [. . .] You're not exercising that discretion?

A. No. [. . .]

Q. How does TransUnion instruct its employees to process the dispute?

A. In the system.

Q. By taking the consumer's dispute, summarizing it into a claim or dispute code, inputting that into the system and sending that code to the creditor?

A. Correct.

Q. Is there any other part of an investigation besides that that TransUnion has instructed its employees is required?

A. No.

As the report and court records indicated, Equifax's procedures are substantially similar. In a March 2007 deposition, Equifax's vice president of global consumer services described that bureau's "reinvestigation" process accordingly:

Q: What knowledge do you have as to the mechanics of how a DDC Filipino employee would process an Equifax dispute? [. . .]

A: The electronic image would be displayed on their screen. They would have an ACIS [Automated Consumer Interview System] screen that they would use. They would then look at the electronic image. They would read off the identifying information, enter [. . .] that ID information into the system, access that credit report. At that point, they'd be able to determine if they were looking at the correct file. If they were, they'd go further. They'd read the letter, they gain an understanding of the issues at hand, and they'd look at the credit report to see if the credit report at that time reflects that. If it does, they would send those particular items to the data furnisher or furnishers. They would request that an investigation be started. [. . . .]

Q: Right. But they're not—they're not going to handle whatever response the creditor may provide?

A: That's correct.

Q: Do DDC employees have telephones on their desk?

A: I do not believe so.

Q: As part of their compliance with Equifax's procedures, do DDC's employees telephone consumers as part of conducting a reinvestigation?

A: They do not.

Q: Do they telephone creditors, the furnishers, as part of conducting a reinvestigation?

A: They do not.

Q: Do they telephone anybody from outside DDC or Equifax as part of conducting a reinvestigation of a consumer dispute?

A: They do not.

Q: What about emailing any of those non-Equifax, non-DDC people, creditor, consumer, or third party?

A: They should not be—they do not email them.

Q: And what about fax machines?

A: [. . .] They do not have fax machines either.

Q: Under what circumstances will a DDC employee forward the consumer's actual dispute letter or documents the consumer provided to the furnisher, the creditor, as part of a reinvestigation?

A: A mechanism does not exist to forward the actual documents.

What makes the process so appalling is that the only human intervention by the credit bureaus' employees is to determine the appropriate three-digit code to enter in a computer message to the creditor. The fact that their systems, as described by an Equifax executive, fundamentally cannot comply with the Fair Credit Reporting Act is a travesty of justice for the American consumer. There is no thought given to the information provided by the consumer. Furthermore, no actual information is considered in the investigation at all!

How The E-OSCAR Batch Interface Encourages Illegal Automated Responses

E-OSCAR is the system that allows data furnishers to electronically communicate with credit reporting agencies throughout the dispute process. Once a dispute is entered into the automated system at the credit-reporting agency, the data furnisher is automatically notified of the dispute through their e-OSCAR online communication system. Data furnishers are provided the three-digit dispute code along with details about the consumer. They respond to all disputes directly in the online system, and the data furnishers have thirty days to respond or the item is automatically deleted. The online system appears to be an efficient way to transfer information and to communicate; however, due to minimal information be transmitted it is nearly impossible to understand the full picture of the consumer's dispute. Now, with recent enhancements (Batch Interface) to e-OSCAR, the process has become even more transparently non-compliant with the FCRA.

E-OSCAR offers data furnishers the ability to update via a Batch Interface, which facilitates the processing of large volumes of consumer disputes in an automated electronic format. This enables the data furnishers to further automate the process by establishing *automatic responses* to the consumer disputes. For example, a reporting agency may choose to auto-populate the response fields based on certain criteria, and then the staff has the option to review each one manually prior to submission.

The problem with this interface is that the reporting agencies leave the final review up to the individual clerk. There is usually no requirement to even review the consumer dispute, although this is clearly required by law. As most employees are overworked and underpaid, most of the consumer disputes will probably not be reviewed by an actual live person. Once again, this benefits the data furnishers and credit bureaus alike.

The Batch Interface itself is not a violation of the FCRA, as data furnishers are free to do with the information what they wish, without fear of repercussions. When the information is not reviewed, but automated, there is a clear violation of the FCRA.

In other words, they're just providing the tools to break the law. Despite this disclaimer, there's really no legally compliant reason to have the Batch Interface in the first place. The FCRA mandates each dispute be investigated, but then the reporting agencies empower the data furnishers with tools to avoid having to do an actual investigation. This is a distribution of responsibility where everyone involved gets to avoid the blame, and it's transparently unfair to the little guy.

Chapter 7: The Cost of Correcting Errors

Consider this true story: Jeanette A. Davis files for bankruptcy. Johnette A. Davis is her daughter who has moved from the family home several years prior. Despite the fact that their first names, date of birth, social security numbers, and current addresses are different, Jeanette's bankruptcy data is reported on Johnette's credit file.

While the mistake was correctable, it took a significant amount of time to correct. It also created problems for the daughter who was in the process of purchasing a home. Needless to say, the home purchase was put on hold until the mess could be straightened out.

If Johnette would have had all of her mother's negative credit information erroneously reported on her credit report, she would need to expend a tremendous amount of time fighting to have it removed. Like most consumers, Johnette would have to make the decision about what information was worth removing and what information is simply not worth the time and effort.

One of the biggest flaws in the credit system is that the burden of proof is on the consumer, not the creditor or collection agency. Considering these errors don't originate from the consumer, this is 100% backwards. The system allows the creditors to add information to a consumer credit report without having to provide any proof that the item is valid. Once the item is on the credit report, the consumer must provide proof that the item is incorrect. If a creditor reports an account that is not the customer's, the dispute is very difficult to resolve because the consumer is unable to produce proof that the account is not theirs. In this instance, the creditor holds the consumer's good credit hostage as they wait for a response.

Even when a response is provided, the creditor's word is what is considered fact, not the consumer's complaint. This process allows creditors to report inaccurate information on consumer credit reports at an alarming rate. In one landmark case, Johnson v. MBNA, the plaintiff's attorney learned from MBNA's account records that the consumer was expressly told, "It is not our burden to prove you owe the debt. It is your burden to prove you do not." Clearly, the consumer is unable to provide information proving that they do not own the debt, except in the case of Jeanette and Johnette. The situation this mother and daughter found themselves in is the exception rather than the rule. When information from another account winds up on your report, odds are you will never know the real source.

For the consumer, there are two choices: pay off the amount to improve their credit report or ignore the item and pay higher interest rates. In some instances, the errors are so egregious that the consumer is unable to obtain a line of credit at all.

To correct credit report errors, the consumer must dispute the same item multiple times. If the consumer has the financial means to do so, they will hire an attorney to assist with the process. There are some consumers with the tenacity, time, and education level to efficiently file and manage multiple disputes at once. Still, many creditors and collection agencies will not respond until they see a letter from an attorney.

The example of Jeanette and Johnette is an example of *a mixed/merged credit file,* which occurs when the information from two separate peoples' credit files somehow become merged. With the sophisticated computer systems in place to manage the data, one would assume that this was a rare occurrence, but sadly it is not.

In instances where two consumers have similar names, social security numbers, addresses, or birth dates, a mixed/merged credit file is a highly probable occurrence, rather than a rare one. This is what occurred when Jeanette's and Johnette's files became merged. The data indicates that out of the total number of occurrences 64% of the merged information came from total strangers, while 36% came from a relative or former spouse. The type of situation outlined above occurs naturally, as a byproduct of the inherent flaws which exist in the current system.

A special type of ID theft exists called "Synthetic ID Theft" that takes advantage of this "feature" of the credit system. With synthetic ID theft a thief mixes fake information with real or partially real information from an unsuspecting victim. This often results in a new credit file being created for the fraudster, and the subsequent negative information eventually being merged into the consumer's file, which of course harms their credit.

How can the IRS and other large agencies store accurate data, while the credit reporting agencies cannot? The reason is that the credit reporting bureaus do not use rigorous and conclusive data matching processes to match the data with any accuracy. While the credit bureaus could easily implement a better matching system they have no motivation to do so. Herein lies another practice that injures the consumer.

How exactly do the sloppy data matching practices of the credit bureaus hurt consumers? This book makes a pretty good case for this if you put it all together, but let me summarize the issue by saying this: Sloppy data matching means more false positives, which means more mixed/merged credit files, which means more "ID Theft" complaints and inaccurate credit reports, which means more consumers struggling to fix their credit and having trouble along the way. It also means that it's just plain easier for ID theft to take place. Make no mistake about it, the credit bureaus' "partial match" algorithms hurt consumers!

"Then why do they do it," you ask? Because more stringent matching requirements would eventually mean more stringent reporting requirements, which for the credit bureaus would ultimately mean <u>LESS</u> data and therefore <u>LESS</u> MONEY.

Not to mention that if the credit bureaus implemented a system that required an eight- or nine-digit match, they would lose some of the efficiencies that enable quick data transfer, and that in turn would reduce profits. Here is an example. It is a common practice of major department stores to offer customers instant credit at the checkout. Currently, the system allows for a partial match of the Social Security number and some additional data that is provided by the consumer. If the system required an eight- or nine-digit match, the data would not be transferred as quickly and in many instances, no match would be found. This would require the clerk to call the credit bureau to find out why they did not obtain a match and to remedy the situation live.

The additional time required to do this extra step would not facilitate the instant credit at the checkout process. More importantly, the credit bureaus would lose money, as they would be selling less data. This is only one example as mortgage companies, banks, credit card companies and auto dealerships all rely on this instant data feature to do their everyday business.

Surely the Creditors Want Accurate Information?

One would assume that the creditors would want to base their lending decisions on the most accurate information. After all, they are in the business of calculated risk and accuracy stands to lower their risk, right? Well, not exactly. Creditors actually benefit when there are errors on the consumers' credit report.

For example, a woman applies for a car loan. She has 25% down and seeking to borrow a conservative amount of money in relation to the salary she makes. Her credit report is pulled by the car dealership. While she appears to have very good credit, it is not good enough to qualify her for a promotional rate of 0%. She is offered the car loan at a 6.9% standard interest rate instead.

If the approval process were not automated and actually required a manual review of her credit report, she may have the opportunity to identify the items that are incorrect and provide evidence to the dealership to obtain the 0% interest rate. However, the process is automated therefore actual credit reports are rarely reviewed during the process. Chances are that she will purchase the car at the 6.9% interest rate. The auto industry benefits in two ways.

First, they are able to profit from the financing; when a consumer is eligible for a promotional rate (0%, 1.9%, etc) offered by automotive dealers through special financing provided by the manufacturer, the auto dealership does not profit based on the interest rate agreed to; however, when someone does *not* qualify for those special rates, they are able to upsell the interest rates and not only profit from the sale of the car, they can profit from the financing of the car as well.

Secondly, the calculated risk they are taking is actually lower than the credit report indicates, because she is actually a better credit risk than her score indicated!

Synthetic ID Theft: How Does It Happen?

As time goes on, the flawed system enables credit reports to accumulate additional and erroneous personal identifying information. This would include incorrect names, addresses, employers, and Social Security numbers. When one Social Security number is associated with more than one name, a credit sub-file is created. When a woman gets married and changes her name, a sub-file is created. While this example may be reasonable, consider the next one. When John Smith, Jr. fills out a credit application and forgets to put the Jr. at the end of his name, this name variation will also create a credit sub-file as well. Clearly, not so reasonable.

These sub-files exist because the credit reporting agencies verification algorithms allow for partial matching of personal information. This combined with the inability to distinguish between fraudulent and normal variations and consumers' lack of expertise to identify and eliminate these variations laid the groundwork for loopholes that perpetuate a clear path for an identity theft.

With Synthetic ID Theft, an identity thief creates a new identity by combining real and fabricated personal information. The sub-file that is created is not an issue as it is not associated with the consumer's main file. The consumer does not detect the variation, even if the credit report is reviewed. The only way there is an association of the A file with the sub-file is if a potential creditor requests a report that shows every file associated with the Social Security number. Even then, the synthetic identity may not be detected if the information if there is not negative information in that sub-file. In this instance, the sub-file has no bearing on the credit score of the consumer, and is thus a non-issue.

Usually, the only time a consumer is aware of the sub-files that are used to perpetuate synthetic identity theft is when they are denied credit because the identity has maxed out a line of credit and entered into default.

Doesn't Synthetic ID Theft Cost the Credit Reporting Agencies Money?

The answer is no. While it is the credit reporting agencies that set up this system of flaws and loopholes, it is not the credit reporting agencies that bear the cost of this crime. Once again, the consumer comes out on the short end of the stick. It is the consumer who is inconvenienced when they uncover the crime and the consumer who must deal with the aftermath. The creditors also pay the price as the identity thieves will not be coming forward to pay the bills on the credit cards that they have obtained by fraud.

Commonly Overlooked Problems

Most consumers fail to recognize these variations in their credit reports and they are commonly overlooked as a result. Even the most conscientious consumer will probably not know how to identify these variations that cause the sub-files to be created. Given the challenges and obstacles associated with correcting inaccurate information on credit files, most consumers are apt to concentrate on the items that are a high priority.

Lending professionals have been telling consumers for years to only concentrate on those items on their credit report, which negatively affect their credit scores. In addition, most consumers are not well versed on how to read a credit report so errors will appear to be within acceptable limits. For example, a misspelling of a name would be considered a low priority as it has no real bearing on the consumer's credit score.

Difficult for the Consumer to Correct

If anything has become clear by now, it should be that the consumer is the last consideration in the credit reporting process. Despite the FCRA, numerous consumer watchdog groups and no shortage of attorneys ready and willing to take on the Big Three credit reporting agencies, the credit reporting agencies are not going to change the way they manage our credit data. Therefore, it is up to consumers to protect themselves from synthetic ID theft. This is easier said than done, however. There are a series of steps and a specific skill set necessary to correct these variations. While some consumers are highly proficient in most areas of their life, most find themselves ill-equipped and unable to efficiently correct the errors that allow the identity thief to run rampant with their identity.

- First, the consumer needs to know how to read the report to determine what information is unnecessary or more importantly, erroneous.

- Then the consumer would need a crystal ball to fully understand the risk for leaving each piece of information on their credit report instead of requesting that it be removed.

- Finally, the consumer needs to know who to write about the information and how to request that it be removed from the credit report.

- Recall the convenient three-digit code that the credit reporting agencies use. Which one is the right code? How does the consumer get the credit bureau to look at their backup information and notes?

- Even if the consumer is well versed in these areas, then there is one final step, the variation elimination process. Once again, the credit reporting agencies set the rules without regard for anyone but themselves.

As an example, investigations conducted by Equifax have proven to remove the disputed PII (personal identifying information), but they provide no means for the consumer to verify that all of the erroneous information has been removed. All three major credit bureaus offer varying reports that attempt to reconcile the claim, but when the totality of the report is considered, the results contradict each other.

Consider the following canned response that is generated from one of the three bureaus when a consumer attempts to eliminate the erroneous PII:

> *"We have reviewed the identification information. The results are: Your name has been updated. You may wish to provide your credit grantors with the update. These items have been updated per the information you have supplied."*

This statement denotes the only information contained in the file are the Name, SSN and birthdate as precisely listed; however, later in the report, and camouflaged, is a section Formerly Known As which does not merely refer to maiden names. Also contained in this section are Previous Address(es) It appears the space only permits five addresses; thus, it is difficult to determine if there are additional, non-listed addresses contained in the file."

This reply is misleading at best. It on the surface leads the consumer to believe that the information has been reviewed and updated; however, later information in the report would indicate that no such update has truly taken place. What's going on here?

Flaws In the System

Despite the laws that exist to protect consumers, the current credit reporting system has glaring flaws. As credit is necessary to navigate the current economy, these flaws can keep average citizens from purchasing a car, getting a job, and establishing utility services. Despite the fact that these flaws are well documented and constantly disputed, they continue to exist. It might even be said that the flaws actually make the current system fundamentally unsound, as they are so detrimental to the consumers and finance companies they claim to serve.

Shockingly, the credit bureaus' high-paid lobbyists spread the message that credit repair is illegal and an abuse of the system. To cloud the issue even further, the credit bureaus claim that credit repair companies are scams that defraud consumers and create more problems than they resolve. The credit bureaus attempt to partner with the FTC in an attempt to crack down on credit repair companies. The measures they are trying to put in place will literally cripple the consumer's ability to repair credit inaccuracies. Those in the industry of credit repair are aware that there are some bad apples that need to be cleaned up, but the true cleanup that's needed is on the part of the credit bureaus. It's fairly obvious from what we've discussed to this point that the credit bureaus are continually breaking the law, and soon you'll see the real complaint statistics to show how the *so-called* bad-guy credit repair companies compare in complaints to the Big Three.

Each bureau obviously supports its own interests and has an agenda. Until now, consumers have had no voice of their own.

An off-the-record comment was made by one of the top international providers of merchant services [the people who make it possible for businesses to accept credit cards as payment]. The comment stated that the FTC was putting tremendous pressure on the merchant services companies to *not accept* credit repair companies as clients.

The FTC's rationale was attributed to undocumented high charge back, return and complaint rates. The major international company combated the statements by saying their credit repair company's portfolio statistics are in line with their overall portfolio. This is just another example of the credit bureaus and government agencies wrongfully denying consumers the ability to fight back. Good people who want to help consumers are often scared away from entering this industry because of its draconian rules that ultimately injure the consumer, because the consumer doesn't have sufficient choices to get professional help.

Chapter 8: Secrets of the Mortgage Lending Industry

Credit Resellers

Another primary source of income for the credit bureaus is reselling reports for potential real estate purchases. The bureaus typically do not directly sell report to banks, loan officers, or mortgage brokers. Instead, resellers contract with the credit bureaus to provide a compilation of data from all three bureaus, commonly known as a *trimerge report.* This is all good on the face of it, except for the fact that trimerge reports have the highest amount of errors and much lower data matching requirements than a consumer report.

In anticipation of a home purchase, the consumer will evaluate their own credit, work hard to maintain a positive history, and continually monitor that positive history so they can simply walk into their local bank to apply for a loan. When they get to the bank they find out that there are many negative items on their credit report that did not show up when they pulled the consumer version of the report. As a result, the consumer is either improperly denied a loan, or is forced to pay a higher interest rate.

The resellers are contracted with the credit bureaus and as part of their contract with banks, loan officers, and mortgage brokers, they often include verbiage in their contract that restricts the banks, loan officers or mortgage brokers from providing or referring any consumer to a credit repair company, or assisting a consumer to repair their credit. The language is so restrictive that a bank, loan officer, or mortgage broker could permanently lose their ability to resell credit reports from that reseller or in general if they help a consumer legally repair their credit, or refer them to a legal credit repair business.

As is a common theme throughout this exposé, the credit bureaus do not want consumers to repair their credit and don't want qualified licensed people (the mortgage lenders) advising on credit repair. The worse your credit is, the more money the credit bureaus make.

The credit bureaus do allow for one type of consumer defense to the trimerge trap called *rapid rescoring*, where the reseller typically contests just a few well-chosen items for a fee of $30 to $90 per item. They usually achieve resolution within 72 hours. The cost for the repairs then become part of the closing costs and may result in saving thousands of dollars over the course of a loan. The resellers are allowed to sell ancillary products to loan officers, bankers, mortgage lenders to analyze scores and they provide rapid rescoring processes.

Wait a minute! Seventy-two-hour resolution? The consumer and many legitimate credit repair companies are unable to get an answer within 30 days, but the resellers, who enable to CRAs to make millions of dollars, can get responses within 72 hours. Sounds like the credit reporting agencies have found yet another way to profit from their own incompetence! The credit reporting agencies should be *paying* the consumers because they had errors; they shouldn't be able to *profit* from their errors. Based on rapid rescore and all the other items we've covered in this book, it should be apparent that the credit bureaus' profits increase as the consumers credit decreases! It's also much clearer now why the credit bureaus don't like credit repair companies: *they don't want the competition!*

Let us be clear: the situation is highly unethical and should be illegal. The bureaus and resellers are contractually forcing the mortgage broker/lender/banker into performing malpractice. The banker/lender has a fiduciary responsibility to the consumer, but they neglect to fulfill this responsibility because they are in fear of losing their contract with their reseller. They should be helping consumers in any way possible, either by referral to a qualified credit specialist, or by assisting the consumer on their own. Due to contractual restrictions, they withhold from referring or providing a service that consumers need. With the wide acceptance and knowledge of the significant amount of credit errors that exist on most credit reports, forcing professionals to withhold referrals or advice by threatening to take away their livelihood (credit pulling privileges) should be considered a crime.

When a consumer legally disputes an item on their report, the Fair Credit Reporting Act mandates that the data furnisher mark the item as "in dispute." This way if someone is applying for credit, the potential new creditor will be warned that the consumer is disputing the item, and they can make their underwriting judgment call based on the information provide. Due to the automation of the banking system, underwriting systems, and approval systems over the past several years, it is rare for an actual underwriter to make a decision. As with so many of our everyday processes, a computer actually makes the underwriting decision to approve you for a loan.

These advanced systems were supposed to be much more accurate and efficient than human underwriters. Furthermore, the automated decisions were supposed to be far superior. And yet, just a few short years after automated underwriting became the norm, the banking system had collapsed, with the highest amount of defaults in human history. In 2009, we saw 157 banks fail; these are not the kind of record numbers anybody wanted to see. Clearly, the automated underwriting is not the panacea as the bean counters claimed it to be. In fact, it has turned into a horror show, but they won't admit it.

The credit reporting agencies refuse to remedy the situation and will not admit fault with the automated systems in place. The automated underwriting system, combined with the government's policies, completely strip consumers of their legal rights, forcing them to be enslaved by the credit industry and accept absorbent fees, costs, and interest. It is commonplace for the injured consumer to accept the illegal and erroneous items on their credit when applying for a mortgage. What choice do they have?

Add to that the monopoly and insider dealings between the credit bureaus and resellers to drain consumers of unnecessary monies by charging more fees, and collecting more credit report costs, and the consumer is a virtual hostage.

The newest insult and injury to the consumer is the manner in which the federal government is aiding the bureaus in the continual perpetration of this fraud on the consumer.

The vast majority of all residential mortgages in today's market are originated through one of the existing government loan programs, whether it be Fannie Mae, Freddie Mac, USDA, VA, or FHA. They all have implemented similar automated underwriting guidelines and processes. While the lending manuals for all of these programs state that a manual review is possible, actually getting one is another story. Most loan officers, bankers, and mortgage brokers have neither seen nor have requested a manual review on any of these programs, which means that they are left for automated approval only.

What is not common knowledge is the fact that the automated review process is programmed to automatically deny any loan file of a consumer who has any items noted as "in dispute" on their credit reports. Therefore, while the federal government and the FTC publicly support consumer rights and pass legislation such as the FCRA, their actions deny consumers fundamental rights that are afforded for in the FCRA. This once again leaves consumers alone, injured, frustrated, and as we will see in the Kenneth Baker case, desperate to the point of taking extraordinary measures.

So how does a regular person get a home loan?

Let's recap the situation thus far. The credit reports used to obtain a home mortgage are not the ones that the consumer receives from the credit reporting agencies. They are instead reports sold by credit resellers that merge the credit information from all three CRAs into the trimerge. This trimerge has a lower standard of matching than even the consumer version of the report and contains significantly more errors as a result. The consumer is never allowed to view this trimerged report. The consumer is not told what specific items are being used to approve their mortgage loan because underwriting uses an automated process that a real, live, breathing, person has not part in completing. If the consumer does get wind of the errors on their credit file and chooses to dispute the items so they are weighted differently in the underwriting process (which is their right under the FCRA), the loan will automatically be denied by any government mortgage loan program.

Despite the situation described above, loans are being successfully underwritten every day. How, you may ask? Well, the consumers who are successfully obtaining federal home loans are simply accepting the situation for what it is and giving up. Instead of disputing errors on their credit report, they are simply not disputing the illegally reported data. This means that they incur higher costs and much worse, higher interest rates over the term of the loan. While a viable strategy may be to get into the loan and then refinance down the road if and when the negative items can be disputed and removed, the additional costs associated with signing a less-than-optimum mortgage loan can be in the thousands. Is it really worth it?

For some consumers, it may be worth the time and effort to take this strategy. After all, it is a buyer's market and nothing can beat the reduced prices that the foreclosure market is offering. Besides, if the consumer just sits and waits around for a few years, surely the items will age out and fall off their report right? Wrong! Items that are a result of incorrect file matching and reporting errors will not fall off. In fact, there may be more erroneous items on the consumer's credit report each time the reseller performs a trimerge. The consumer will never have the opportunity to see the errors as the lender will not share the trimerged report so there is no sure-fire way for the consumer to create a plan to improve on this no-win situation.

Dispute an Item, Pay the Price

Despite the consumer protection laws that empower consumers with ability to dispute, doing so locks them out of government mortgage programs, as the automated underwriting system will not accept credit files with items in dispute.

If the consumer does dispute an item, the data furnishers have a method of payback for consumers exercising their rights.

Even after a disputed item investigation is complete, the data furnishers continue to report the dispute as active. The consumer is really stuck between a rock and a hard place. Let's say that the consumer is patient enough to wait the unreasonable amount of time that it takes to fix the errors found in the tri-merged reports that were issued to the bank. They receive the results of the investigation and are ready to accept whatever the decision and move on. But the data furnishers still report the items as "in dispute," which will still trigger an automated denial of their mortgage application.

If the consumer is very ambitious and disputes the "in dispute" verbiage, they do this by opening a *new* dispute! This means that the item is still in dispute, and the automated denial is still in play. The consumer's answer to this is going back to the data furnisher and have them change the status—but the fact is, that is more aggravation that consumers should not be put through.

The FTC: Protecting America's Consumers?

Taken from the FTC consumer complaint site:

"The Federal Trade Commission, the nation's consumer protection agency, collects complaints about companies, business practices, identity theft, and episodes of violence in the media. Your complaints can help us detect patterns of wrong-doing, and lead to investigations and prosecutions. The FTC enters all complaints it receives into Consumer Sentinel, a secure online database that is used by thousands of civil and criminal law enforcement authorities worldwide. The FTC does not resolve individual consumer complaints."

The FTC is hailed as the consumer watchdog, fighting for the protection of consumer rights. Consumers turn to the FTC for advice on the credibility of businesses, scams, fraud, and anything consumer related. The FTC's authority is far reaching. They impose sanctions, keep solicitors from calling you, and give the consumers a warm and fuzzy feeling of security in a very insecure world.

Well, not really. As we will see, the FTC is unwilling to effectively correct the credit and consumer reporting industry in a manner that truly offers the consumer protection.

When the consumer is injured by the credit reporting agencies, credit resellers, or credit card companies, the FTC will not address the individual consumer's complaint. There is a reporting link on the FTC site where a consumer can lodge a complaint, but it clearly states that the FTC *does not* resolve individual consumer complaints. Then what do they do with the information and why would we provide it? If two hundred consumers are injured by FCRA violations by one of the CRAs, how do they get resolution? Do they hire an attorney? How many complaints constitute a big enough issue for the FTC to take action?

The fact is that billions of pieces of data are handled by the credit bureaus monthly. They have little reward for having accurate data because there is a *huge* upside for having negative data on consumers. The system could easily be fixed, but no one is standing up for consumers. The legislators are rarely presented with the facts, and when they are, the lobbyists from the other side twist the truth and downplay the situation. Without exception, every report ever presented to the FTC on accuracy in credit reporting has proven that there is a significant problem with the credit reporting system. Where is the FTC in this equation? Clearly, they are unwilling to do their job.

Chapter 9: Stopping the Insanity

Despite the fact that all of the information and statistics presented in this book are available to the public, most people have no understanding of the situation at hand. Consumers simply accept the situation for what it is. They may complain and get angry at their specific situation, but in reality they feel completely helpless. This is why I've made it my life's work to unify leaders in the credit repair industry in an effort to stop the insanity and change the system. Let me tell you, it has *not* been easy.

The FTC and Credit Bureaus Launch Their Attack

Credit repair companies exist to serve the consumer in correcting inaccurate and erroneous information on credit reports. There are unethical credit repair companies, but in general, there are far more legitimate organizations whose goal is to correct the information on credit reports. Despite the legitimate service the credit repair companies provide, the FTC and the attorney general's office have launched an aggressive campaign warning consumers about the credit repair industry. They go so far to advise the public to repair their own credit reports.

The secretive nature of credit scoring algorithms, along with the automated dispute process, makes it difficult for the average consumer to truly fix their credit on their own. In a recent study by the FTC, an attorney (who was employed by the FTC) was assigned the task of correcting a consumer's credit file. The attorney anonymously worked with the credit reporting agencies and creditors to assess the difficulty of an average person to correct errors on their credit report. Despite his training as an attorney and years of education/training working at the FTC, he was unsuccessful in correcting the inaccuracies on the consumer's credit report. Given the outcome of the study, you may ask yourself, why would government agencies, like the FTC, and attorneys general continue to advise consumers not to hire experts to repair their credit?

Curiously, in fact, the FTC does not openly come out to consumers in any other industry in this manner. They do not say, "You should mow your lawn yourself," or "You should do your own bankruptcy." There is not one other instance where the FTC advises consumers to stay clear from a particular industry or service. However, dealing with your financial future, they have the audacity to tell people to attempt to fix it themselves... and to do so without having proper training and knowledge of the intricate system that is designed to make it nearly impossible for a consumer to get inaccurate information removed from their credit reports. Why, you might ask? The only possible explanation for this is *money*—and lots of it. Yes, I will have the guts to come out and call it the way it is when no one else will: Money is the reason it all happens. How can I be so sure you may ask? Easy.

Years ago, the Big Three bureaus got together and lobbied governmental officials to ban credit repair and to spread propaganda about credit repair companies. This was a focused, organized smear and fear campaign designed to put the credit repair industry out of business. This resulted in the draconian policies of the CROA (Credit Repair Organizations Act) and the TSR

(Telemarketing Sales Rules) which make it difficult for credit repair companies to operate because they have no way to guarantee payment from consumers. Legislators disguised these acts as consumer protection, but in reality they harm consumers by putting small businesses out of business and making it difficult for ethical companies to operate. These various state and federal regulations could have been better serving to consumers by making a national licensing standard (like bankers have) in lieu of simply trying to put them out of business by making them wait to collect their money months after the service has been complete, with no way to force a consumer to pay.

So why would the credit reporting agencies go to such lengths to put the credit repair companies out of business? Because the more people who have bad credit, the more money they make, and there is another way that the credit reporting agencies have found to monetize the dispute process, one I actually feel is a deliberate attempt to monopolize the credit repair industry. We'll talk about that in a bit, but an obvious piece of evidence that shows the FTC is conspiring with the credit bureaus is the list of top complaints that they publish annually.

From the 2011 report:

RANK	CATEGORY	COMPLAINTS	PERCENT
1	Identity Theft	279,259	15%
2	Third Party and Creditor Debt Collection	180,928	10%
3	Prizes, Sweepstakes and Lotteries	100,208	6%
4	Shop-at-Home and Catalog Sales	98,306	5%
5	Banks and Lenders	89,341	5%
6	Internet Services	81,805	5%
7	Auto Related Complaints	77,435	4%
8	Impostor Scams	73,281	4%
9	Telephone and Mobile Services	70,024	4%
10	Advance-Fee Loans and Credit Protection/Repair	47,414	3%
11	Foreign Money Offers and Counterfeit Check Scams	43,101	2%
12	Health Care	38,246	2%
13	Mortgage Foreclosure Relief and Debt Management	38,140	2%
14	Credit Cards	37,932	2%
15	Television and Electronic Media	37,404	2%
16	Business Opportunities, Employment Agencies and Work-at-Home Plans	36,111	2%
17	Internet Auction	35,926	2%
18	Travel, Vacations and Timeshare Plans	32,736	2%
19	Credit Bureaus, Information Furnishers and Report Users	30,203	2%

A closer look reveals that # 10 for 2011 is advance-fee loans and credit protection/repair. Credit repair would have not made this list on its own if it were not combined with advance fee loans. Advance fee loans are payday loans that typically charge 30% or more per month in interest. Despite the fact that there is absolutely no correlation between the two industries, they combined them.

Obviously credit protection/repair would have never made it on the list if it were not combined with another industry. Furthermore, out of all the industries that could have combined it with, they choose payday advance loans, which are notorious for their unethical practices. Thanks, FTC!

The greatest complaint to the FTC, for all of 2011, is identity theft! Despite the fact that ID theft is preventable if only the credit bureaus would be more concerned about the consumer than their profits, the FTC continue to turn a blind eye.

It is also no coincidence that debt collectors, credit card companies and the credit bureaus, if combined, would outrank ID theft. Combining these would make more sense than advance fee loans and credit repair.

Also on the list is debt collectors, which report information to credit bureaus, and often infract the law by reporting information that is unverifiable, outdated, and inaccurate, but the FTC is not quick to say don't do business with a debt collector even though they have over 180,000 complaints. They don't pick on debt collectors or credit bureaus as much as they attack credit repair because of the size of the industry. Simply put, it's another tale of David and Goliath. The credit repair industry does not have any uniformity or voice on Capitol Hill; they have no lobbying effort and that is why they are easily attacked.

Even though credit repair and restoration is a service that is growing in need as economic times get tougher, they constantly get stepped on.

This is yet another reason why I have launched the credit industry's first national non-profit organization to help spread the real word about credit, and credit repair, and to help educate consumers the right way to repair their credit, and understand their legal rights.

Better Business Bureau: A For-Profit Extortion Group

These words may seem harsh, but the truth hurts. For years, the Better Business Bureau (BBB) has disguised itself as an altruistic, government-sanctioned agency, existing to protect the consumer. They claim to police businesses by providing a forum for consumers to report complaints and a rating system for the member businesses.

In reality, the BBB does not police anyone. They actually extort money from businesses by setting up a system that implies that businesses that are not members are less credible and trustworthy.

The BBB consists of local offices that are independently governed by their own boards of directors but are "monitored" nationally by the Council of Better Business Bureaus. The majority of their income is derived from annual membership fees, paid by the businesses they report on. As a business grows, the extortion money increases because the BBB's accreditation costs are determined by the size of the business. These costs range from several hundred to several thousand dollars a year.

Some might argue that the accreditation fees are used to support the activities of the BBB. It might also be plausible to say that the larger the company, the more resources that are required to do what the BBB does. Well, perhaps, but not when you consider the actual rating system that the BBB uses. After all, the only way a company can earn an A+ rating is to be a member.

For example, a business that has been in existence for twenty years and has never acted unethically and always resolved all customer complaints responsibly is unable to receive an A+ rating if they do not pay the extortion money to the BBB. Clearly, it is a pay-to-play situation with the BBB. Given consumers' limited understanding of the BBB, the consumer will assume that the company with the A+ rating is better than the one with a lesser rating or no rating. The truth is that is the BBB's rating system is based on how much money you pay them.

It could also be possible that as this business continues to grow, they determine that the $2,000 membership fee is not a good way to spend their money. Once again, the consumer assumes that all good businesses will be BBB members and there must be something wrong with a large entity that is not associated with the BBB. So to recap, if you pay the BBB their annual extortion fees, your business is protected and possibly rated A+. If you do not wish to submit to the BBB's extortion tactics, your business is penalized.

The BBB of course sees no reason to correct the public's perception of the situation. Why would they? After all, they are in the business to make money—period. If their scam were uncovered, they would have no credibility and consumers would cease to turn to them for information.

The Systematic Attack on the Credit Repair Industry

As we have already discussed, the FTC has already taken a position against the credit repair industry. Along with the credit bureaus, they are on a witch-hunt to discredit and destroy the credit repair industry. This highly focused and well-funded public relations campaign began over twenty years ago when the credit repair industry was enabling millions of consumers to defeat the credit reporting industry's unfair and inaccurate reporting practices. The Big Three credit bureaus responded by partnering with the FTC in a campaign to put the credit repair industry out of business.

The campaign portrays the credit repair industry as unscrupulous vultures who take upfront money before services are performed and then keep that money even if they are unable to clear up your credit. The truth is that most credit repair companies are honest. The credit bureaus use delay tactics to delay the results of the credit repair companies, in efforts to simultaneously maximize their profits and hurt the credit repair companies.

The credit repair industry is simply unable to compete with the deep pockets of the lobbyists. The credit reporting agencies were not going to sit back and let the credit repair industry force them to clean up their act. We already covered how inaccurate credit information makes the credit bureaus more money and how reporting accurately costs them more money. Only those who know this insider information can easily see that the credit repair industry is a threat to the credit reporting agencies. The general public is misled to believe that the FTC regulations and credit bureaus are working to protect them.

Now, not only do small credit repair businesses have to jump through numerous hoops and comply with stringent regulations, but they also now can't get paid until the job is done. It is a wonder that small credit repair companies can stay in business. But the American entrepreneur is resilient. The credit repair industry responded by working with the regulations and still turning a profit. They learned how to draft documents that met the expectation of outlining services and offering a fair contract, thus allowing them to continue to do business. The credit repair industry lived to fight another day on behalf of the consumer. The credit reporting agencies were not happy, so they have persisted until this day, spreading their propaganda and tarnishing an industry that is truly committed to the rights of the consumer.

If the consumer were truly the beneficiary of the past twenty years of this witch hunt, wouldn't someone have investigated the credit reporting agencies, and done more than a slap on the wrist with their findings? After all, they cannot seem to report information correctly or correct the information when they learn that it is inaccurate. If any other business operated with such inaccuracy and benefited financially from it, the FTC would be holding congressional hearings on CSPAN, CNN, and FOX 24/7 until the business was out of business.

Furthermore, if the BBB actually cared about the consumer, wouldn't they be giving the credit bureaus a failing grade? Wouldn't the BBB be doing their duty to defend the consumer by warning them of the unscrupulous practices of the credit reporting agencies? After all, consumers purchase credit monitoring products and credit reports from the bureaus; shouldn't the BBB be warning consumers not to buy credit monitoring products because the credit bureaus profit from their own inaccuracy? Shouldn't the BBB be telling consumers to stop worrying about monitoring their credit if they can simply put a credit freeze on their file which only costs $5 instead of the monthly fees they pay for the monitoring? Why does the BBB not step in?

The answer is clear. The credit bureaus have grown too powerful to stop. It sounds sensational, but it is a cold hard fact. In people's minds they are no different than the IRS. People hate them and hate what they do, but will do nothing to change the current situation. The BBB has everyone fooled into thinking that they are the good guys and are thus not held accountable for their extortion practices. If you think about it, both agencies operate like organized crime syndicates.

The Consumer Isn't Considered in the Equation

According to the credit reporting agencies, *the consumer is not a customer*. We have already discussed how the credit reporting agencies make their money selling data and on the dispute process. The credit bureaus customers are banks, financial institutions, insurance companies, and those who purchase the credit data from the credit bureaus.

The consumer isn't considered. Their well being, their credit rating, nor their best interest is considered at any point. Again, it is not in the credit bureaus' best interests to work with the consumer to correct errors on their credit reports. As the credit repair industry has made great strides in helping these consumers, it is no surprise that the credit bureaus recommend consumers to repair their own credit and not use credit repair companies. The propaganda war that has been waged against the credit repair industry by the FTC, BBB and the three credit bureaus reduces the consumer to a casualty.

The consumer is told that the credit repair industry is the enemy, yet no one has educated the consumers on how to truly protect themselves. Furthermore, most consumers are ill informed about credit data in general.

Consider the following information.

In May of 2007 CFA and Washington Mutual conducted a study on consumer awareness of the credit scoring system. The results of the study are as follows:

Understood that their credit score would increase when they paid off large balances	65 %
Understood that married couples don't have combined scored	57%
Understood that maxing out revolving account would hurt their scores	56%
Knew that there are more than one score	45%
Were able to name the three major CRAs	23%
Believed their income affected their score	74%

Why are these myths perpetrated? The answer is simple. An educated and well-informed consumer base will force the credit bureaus to clean up their act. Education is power when placed in the hands of the people. The credit repair industry is educated. They are informed. They have the credit reporting agencies running scared. Join us in this fight!

FTC Regulatory Enforcement Has Declined Over Time

When the FCRA was enacted, the consumer gained substantial rights. The statue was a powerful piece of legislation that made the credit reporting agencies take notice. Between 1991 and 2000, the FCRA packed a powerful punch, prosecuting all three of the credit reporting agencies and obtaining multiple injunctions in the process. Mixed file issues were addressed and additional FTC resources were assigned to address CRA complaints. Consumers celebrated their victory over the Big Three credit reporting agencies, but the victory was short lived, as the FTC has been largely silent ever since.

While many consumers have sought monetary remedies in court, only the FTC has the power to force any lasting systematic changes for all consumers. The FTC has also failed to act against the credit reporting agencies by challenging the reporting that is required by FACTA. The most important of these, the FTC/FRB Joint Reinvestigation Report concluded hesitantly that there may not be a problem with the reinvestigation process. The FTC failed to seek out more substantive contributions from consumers and the organizations that represent them, again failing to do its job, and leaving the consumer high and dry.

Credit Card Accountability Responsibility and Disclosure Act (CARD)

The most recent exercise in futility is the Credit Card Accountability Responsibility and Disclosure Act (CARD). The CARD act claims that it brings new protections to consumers to save them from the evil credit card companies. These measures are designed to help consumers avoid actions that will lead to negative credit.

An End to Deceptive Marketing Tactics

We all have heard those free credit report commercials offering you a free credit report so you can be sure that no one is stealing your identity. What they do not tell you is that the report isn't free! You must sign up for a very expensive credit monitoring service in order to receive the report. The report is also not the same credit report that is used by lenders when making a credit decision.

The new laws continue to allow these advertisements and claims to be made. They just now offer a disclaimer at the end of the commercial that says, "This is not the free credit report provided for by Federal law." The ethical thing to do would be to require that the commercials are pulled from rotation. Instead, the deception continues and the consumer is hit with yet another disclaimer that they don't pay attention to. The mere fact that the government required the disclaimer is an open admission that the advertisements are misleading and deceptive. The credit bureaus and resellers have found yet another loophole, and since the new disclaimers have hampered their sales they realized that free credit *reports* are prohibited by the new legislation but free credit *scores* aren't. So they've quickly switched all their clever, catchy marketing to push free credit scores, which, somehow, must have been missed by the legislation. Oops—I'm sure that was an accident.

The credit reports that are sent to the consumer are not the same ones that are regularly utilized by the credit reporting agencies. As you recall, the credit reports that are utilized by the credit reporting agencies do not use a full 9/9 match on the Social Security number. These free credit reports do use a 9/9 SS match. The reason is that they do not want to expose the inherent errors in their reports and the file merging problems. They want to instill the fear that some criminal is stealing your identity, not that the credit reporting agencies are giving it away for the sake of easy profits.

If consumers were given the same reports that are given lenders, then consumers would really be flooding the FTC with complaints on the bureaus. They would be absolutely outraged that their credit files are merged and their personal information is mismanaged. This is not the reason behind offering a different report, however. The reason is because the credit reporting agencies make a ton of money playing on the fear of those with good credit that their identities will be stolen. As you recall, the companies offering credit monitoring services are either owned by, or purchase data from, the credit reporting agencies. They want the consumer to think that they still have pristine credit so they get the perfectly matching credit report. What they see is that they still have something of value to protect and they sign up for the credit monitoring service or even worse, consumers will think that their credit is better than it actually is on the report their lenders are seeing! When the consumer decides to go out and purchase something, they will quickly find out that there's a difference between the two reports, but often it's too late because the consumer needs to make that purchase *now*. Therefore, once again, they wind up paying far more than they actually have to.

Improved Monthly Statements

The new law requires the credit card companies to educate the customer about the minimum monthly payment. Specifically, how long it will take to pay off the balance if they pay the minimum payment and the interest that they will pay if they pay the minimum payment over the term of the loan. In this author's opinion, this is old news and a slap in the face to the consumer.

At one time, the minimum monthly payment option was truly deceiving the consumer into thinking that they were doing the fiscally responsible thing to reduce their debt. Over the years, it has become common knowledge that paying only the minimum is a slow death, where you eventually fall behind and then default.

This part of the law is yet another insult to the consumer as the credit card companies should analyze their customer data and focus on educating those consumers who are consistently making the minimum payment, and offering them some financial incentive to pay more. Maybe those customers should be forced to make more than the minimum payment to help them pay down their debt. While these actions might help the consumer, they would reduce the money the credit card companies make from the interest on these customers. It is for this reason, it will never happen. So, once again, we see another useless piece of legislation.

Over-the-Limit Fees Will Be Prohibited

For years, the credit card companies have found new and creative ways to siphon money from the consumer. As if the high interest rates were not enough, they need a little extra icing on the cake to drop to their bottom line. For example, if you have a $25 balance and you are one day over the grace period for making payment, you are charged a $39 late fee. If you go over your limit by $5, you are charged another $39 fee each time you are over the limit. So, if you charge $5 for gas and $20 for groceries, you are charged $39 twice. Over the past ten years, these fees have more than doubled.

This part of the law may be the most deceptive of all. Over-the-limit fees will be prohibited unless consumers explicitly consent to pay for that privilege. In addition, over-the-limit fees may be imposed only one time during the billing cycle, and not for each transaction that exceeds the credit limit. The fees will not be more representative of the situation. For example, the consumer can no longer be charged $39 for going over their limit by only a few dollars. They can be charged $5, however, which begs the question, how is charging the consumer a 100% penalty fee responsible behavior?

In a 2006 Government Accountability Office (GAO) report, the GAO found that the six largest issuers of credit cards "reported that unpaid interest and fees represented about ten percent of the balances owed by bankrupt cardholders." The GAO was not able to obtain from the issuers data on penalty charges these cardholders paid prior to filing for bankruptcy. The GAO also found that fees had doubled in ten years to $34 for late payments and $31 for over-the-limit fees.

Rules Will Require Reductions in Interest Rates

The new legislation addresses the rampant increase in interest fees. Rates hikes for consumers who have had credit issues will need to be reviewed every six months. The problem is that the credit card company will be reviewing itself, not an outside agency. If that sounds like a classic recipe for corruption, that's probably because it is. Any taxpayer should be concerned about a "regulatory" relationship that lazy. If they're going to work for corporations, they should get their salaries paid by them, too.

In the past consumers with short-term credit issues were charged higher interest fees. There was no regulation on this practice and only served to further injure the consumer. Throughout 2008-2009 the credit card companies went on an interest-rate-raising frenzy. There were no rules of engagement. In fact, the consumer was completely blindsided when the rate increases went into effect. There was no explanation, no appeal, no recourse. The interest rate increases were applied to the existing balance that was incurred based on the initial interest agreement, which was lower.

Consider a consumer who is doing their best to keep themselves afloat financially and they are hit with a higher interest rate, with no warning or explanation. The consumer may have meticulously planned to make the payment on time, based on the lower interest rate. Let's say that consumer was struggling financially and unable to afford even a 1% percent interest increase. Too bad for them—if they could not make the new payment, they would incur late fees and over-the-limit fees.

The law also requires that once a consumer's interest rate has been increased, the credit card company must "review" the rate each six months until the rate is lowered to the initial rate. This law does not specify how high the rate can be, the requirements for raising or lowering a rate, or that notifications are provided to consumers that outline the reasons why the rate was not lowered. Again, the law is vague and ambiguous as to how the consumer benefits. The credit card company can simply review the client's file for an indefinite period, but keep the higher interest rate if it feels that it is warranted. As with everything else creditors do, the reviews are expected to be automated.

The reevaluation of rate increases "applies to both increases in annual percentage rates based on factors specific to a particular consumer's creditworthiness, and to increases in annual percentage rates imposed due to factor such as changes in market conditions or the issuer's costs of funds." If after a review it is determined the rate should be reduced, the rule requires the reduction be made within thirty days of the completion of the review.

In addition to requiring a review every six months, credit card companies are required to inform consumers of the reasons for increases in rates. The credit card companies are required to notify the customer why their rate was increased. This is designed to give the consumer the ammunition they need to question the rate increases, and make sure that the six-month reviews are done for the same reasons. The most common example presented is a rate increase that is a result of late payments. Supporters of this legislation make the claim that in this instance, once the consumer has paid on time for six months, the credit card company will be required to reduce the rate.

Here is a more realistic scenario of the application of this piece of legislation. Joe has demonstrated a responsible use of credit by paying his obligations in a timely manner and not living beyond his means. Joe applies for some new credit, which automatically lowers his credit score once the inquiries hit his credit report. The credit card company responds by raising his rate from an introductory rate of 6% to 17%, citing that Joe's debt-to-income ratio is too high and he is now a credit risk.

Joe is notified of this increase and he attempts to appeal this decision. He is stonewalled by the credit card company, transferred to numerous customer service agents, and then finally disconnected. Here is the catch: Joe cannot effectively change his debt-to-income ratio without closing the new accounts and paying off the balances, so he is forced to pay a higher interest rate. The credit card company will comply with the new legislation by doing six-month reviews and holding the rate steady. Joe can complain all he wants to but he has no recourse.

Does this sound familiar? It should, as each and every time the consumer makes any type of advance or obtains additional protections, the credit reporting agencies and credit issuers find a way to circumvent the spirit of the law.

Protection for Young Consumers

Consumers under the age of 21 will only be issued a credit card when they have a co-signer that is over 21 or they can prove that the debt can be repaid. After being a consumer credit advocate for years, this section of the legislation is by far the most egregious display of deception to the consumer.

Credit card companies are high-tech predators who, like the credit reporting agencies, make the most money when the consumer is in over their head and unable to repay their debts quickly. Penalty fees alone reportedly brought in $22.5 billion in 2010. Furthermore, over five percent of all credit card holders are over $8,000 in the hole, with no chance of getting out in today's economy. These same consumers relied on the credit card companies' wisdom to determine how much credit they should be granted based on their stated income. The credit card companies are now required to verify that sufficient income exists to repay the debt for adults between the ages of 18-21.

Sounds great, but it begs the question: why have they not been doing this all along? Does this excuse them of the obligation to responsibly extend credit to those over the age of 21?

Let's think of the reality of this provision and the likely unintended consequences. For years, college campuses have been riddled with credit card application stands. Credit has come easy to students with little or no ability to pay, but the concept of easy money all too often wins the battle against basic logic. Now do you truly think that needing a co-signer will get in the way of students seeking extra cash? Needing a person over 21 to accomplish the task is something most college-aged students have already mastered; just think of the amount of alcohol they consume. Students are quick to find someone over 21 to go buy their alcohol; don't you think it will be easy for them to grab someone over 21 to cosign for their new cash card? That's where the unintended consequences will likely arise. As students procure ripe 21-year-olds to cosign for their first cash card, now the credit card companies actually increase their likelihood to collect, thanks to the second guarantor. Friends might be close in college but as years pass by they typically move on, and will be stuck in the obligations created by a simple signature.

What Is the Point, Anyway?

To be abundantly clear, the CARD act was passed because the media picked up on the earnings reports of the banks and other financial institutions after government bailouts. Upon further investigation of these reports, it was revealed that miscellaneous banking fees (overdraft, late fees, over-the-limit, etc) accounted for a substantial amount of the revenues generated. The public was outraged that the same banks that received billions of dollars in TARP and other government handouts were permitted to conduct business in this manner. The CARD act was drafted as a result. The media chose to focus on only the spirit of the CARD act and inundated the public with news of credit card regulations that would save the public millions of dollars annually. Without any in depth analysis, the public accepted the media's spin on the situation and went about their business.

It Almost Feels Criminal

Consumers are used to being bullied by collection agencies that threaten them over the phone. They threaten to call employers, garnish wages, and even put people in jail. All of which was highly illegal. Then, credit card companies abused the consumer by charging outrageous junk fees. Luckily for us, the CARD act is here to protect unsuspecting consumers from further victimization. When combined, these acts are so egregious that they border on criminal. One behavior which is clearly criminal is the CRA's perpetuation of ID theft to boost profits.

The credit reporting agencies perpetuate ID theft due to their refusal to provide their services responsibility. They add millions of dollars to their bottom line each year by selling services to combat the crimes that they allow to occur. There should be a RICO indictment for the credit bureaus for assisting in an ongoing criminal enterprise, by continuing to allow it to happen, as they are accessories to most true ID theft.

"Willfully negligent" is also the best way to describe the ongoing catastrophe of merged file problems. Now, the story I'm about to relate here is shocking, and it's clearly a "worst case scenario"—but it's also real. All of the problems we're exposing in this report are more than just accounting mistakes; they have real-world consequences that range from inconvenient to devastating. As you're about to find out, they can even turn deadly.

Meet Kenneth Baker

Kenneth Baker was a regular family man who in 2005 had one primary goal: he wanted to move his family into a new home. The family home in Loudoun County, Virginia was too cramped for his wife, daughter, and his wife's children. The purchase of the new home required mortgage approval from a lender. As Kenneth was a fiscally responsible man and paid his bills on time, obtaining a mortgage should have been a reasonably simple process.

As with a fair number of the unsuspecting public, Kenneth's credit history had become mixed or merged with that of another Kenneth Baker—one who was not so diligent about paying his bills. The other Kenneth Baker had a credit history that was so poor that he could not obtain financing on a Hot Wheels car. He had racked up numerous delinquencies, charge-offs, collections and judgments against him.

These black marks showed up on Kenneth Baker's credit report, making it impossible for him to get a mortgage. As is the case with other consumers, Kenneth set out on a quest to correct these errors with the credit reporting agencies. After all, he could easily prove that these were not his items. He spent the next eighteen months sending multiple disputes to the credit bureaus. He spent a significant amount of his savings to hire lawyers to write dispute letters to the bureaus. They explained, over and over, how the other man's negative accounts had gotten mixed into his credit report, how he needed the problem fixed to get a mortgage, and even how the credit bureaus' procedures had caused similar problems in other cases that resulted in successful lawsuits against the bureaus. The attorney cited case law and legal statues, but to no avail.

Not to be defeated, Kenneth repeatedly applied for a home loan—sometimes applying more than once in a month. In good faith, he explained to each mortgage broker how some other man's negative accounts had been mixed into his credit history.

Not surprisingly, the situation took its toll on Kenneth. Feelings of helplessness, anxiety, stress, and depression began to take over his life. The embarrassment was also too much to bear. Kenneth felt like a complete failure and unable to provide for his family.

On March 24, 2006, Kenneth Baker committed suicide. In his last dispute letter to Experian, he wrote of how his battle to fix his credit report had destroyed his life. In his suicide note, Kenneth referred to his ordeal with the credit bureaus.

In this case, inaccurate credit reporting literally cost a man his life.

This is a travesty that easily could have been avoided. The simple steps that we've discussed in this book—ones that the credit reporting agencies should take—could have stopped this from happening. How many other tragedies have taken place due to the negligence of credit reporting agencies? The number is probably staggering, as money and credit seem to revolve around most marital problems. How many marriages could have been saved if they didn't have money problems grinding them down? Often times, better credit = more money = a happier marriage. Obviously money doesn't equal happiness, but it sure makes it a lot easier to be happy when you're not constantly worried about money.

Chapter 10: How You Can Make a Difference

In 2010, the credit industry reached an astounding milestone: Over 25% of US consumers have a credit score lower than 599. This is nothing short of a tragedy, brought on by the real estate crisis and the abusive, broken system that I've been laying out in this book. However, one of my favorite quotes is this gem from Winston Churchill: "A pessimist sees a problem in every opportunity, yet an optimist sees an opportunity in every problem." This is the ultimate opportunity.

In this chapter, I'd like to share with you a road map for getting involved and becoming a part of the solution.

I got involved with credit repair because I saw it as a clear-cut way to make money by actually helping people. I never intended to be an advocate for the entire credit repair industry—I just wanted to start a business and help my clients and friends! Instead, I found my livelihood under attack from corporations worth billions, and watched things get even worse when federal agencies started to join in on the witch hunt. I knew I had to fight back, and I've been teaching the facts and developing solutions ever since.

When I present the average hard-working American citizen with the information here, their reaction is usually the same: they get angry! That's a completely understandable reaction. However, I don't want you to walk away from this book believing that the situation is hopeless. It's absolutely not. We have always overcome those difficulties, and these days I see the situation improving. More and more people are becoming aware of this information because we have the truth on our side!

If you want to get involved and make a difference, I have a suggestion you should consider: perhaps the universe is telling you to start a career in credit repair. It's got the right recipe for a growth market in tough times: huge demand, reliable results, and a low cost of entry.

Of course, nobody should enter into any business on a whim. Getting into the credit repair industry is not a snap decision by any means. On the other hand, though, consider this: having read the material in this book, you're already far more informed than your customers will be. In fact, you're also more informed than most actual employees of the credit reporting agencies are! They can spend an entire career without ever learning the stark facts I've presented here, because they have no incentive to uncover the truth. They're just earning a paycheck, doing a job that basically boils down to supervising computers and answering the occasional phone call.

I'm not going to overstate my case. Business is never "E-Z" and you should be suspicious of those who tell you otherwise. Just the same, after years of helping people get started in this line of work, I can tell you that it's inevitably easier than people think it is. I do keep close track of obscure federal laws, but I'm not a lawyer. The most important qualifications for this line of work are patience, persistence, and a genuine desire to help your clients improve their lives.

I want to see you get involved, but only for the right reasons. I have pushed myself, year after year, to be as honest, ethical and meticulously legal as possible in all aspects of my business. During that time, I've gone from encouraging people to get involved to actually providing the training, the software and the business blueprints that they need to succeed. Through programs like the Credit Repair Boot Camp, I've been answering tough, skeptical questions for years.

Let's get the simplest question out of the way first: the credit repair industry is absolutely not a get-rich-quick plan. I am not doing "Internet marketing," and anyone who promises you easy money for easy work is lying to you. Although DisputeSuite.com makes the process of getting started simpler than it ever was for me, there's still a very real learning curve, and many steps between you and a functional business.

DisputeSuite will also make the day-to-day work of credit repair way more efficient and effective, but it won't be doing the work for you, either. The daily responsibilities remain the same: helping real people with real problems, and doing long-term negotiations with major corporations who want to make life difficult for you. DisputeSuite just keeps you on track, automates your paperwork, and helps you get more done every day than you could possibly manage without it.

Now, I've laid out a strong case against credit card industry lobbyists and even government agencies unfairly targeting and slandering the credit repair industry, but when it comes to regulation, I am all for it. In fact, my advice to anyone starting a credit repair business is to maintain a much higher standard of professionalism and transparency than the law requires. Compliance is just the baseline. Truly professional credit repair agencies provide exceptional service, reliable information and accountable results.

The Bad Guys

I've been in this business for a long time, and I've seen some spectacular failures in my day. Despite the propaganda of the credit reporting agencies and the strange warnings of the FTC, though, I haven't seen that many "bad guys" in this line of work. There's a very simple reason for that: if you want to make fast money by ripping people off and defrauding your customers, there's a long list of industries with a lower barrier to entry and a much simpler business model before you get down to credit repair.

For a scam artist, our industry is simply not worth the work and the setup time.

Just the same, we do have bad guys of a different kind, I'm sad to say. The really serious problems in our industry aren't created by bad intentions; they're created by bad execution. This is why I devote so much of my time to education and outreach. This is also a major reason why I created DisputeSuite: to remove the potential for human error from the equation as much as possible.

What we're going to cover here is a crash course in doing it right. Rather than tantalize you with the thought of building a business, let's lay out a real-world guide to getting it done. You should know exactly what you're in for, especially since there's a good chance it's simpler than you think.

Remember, whatever problems you have and no matter what obstacles you run into, I've been there. I have made mistakes every step of the way, and thanks to those setbacks I've built a system for getting un-stuck, ASAP.

Your Basic Foundation

1. Your Company. You need three core documents to actually be a business. You to set up as an LLC, S or C corporation; you need to register your business with your State's Corporation Registration office; and you need to file for a tax ID number. Without these, you can't technically have a business at all. Additional registration and licensing may be required by your specific state, check DisputeSuite.com for more information regarding state specific licensing requirements.

Pro Tip: when it comes to recommending services, I keep it simple: millions of people use LegalZoom because it always works. You want your costs low and their paperwork is perfect by design.

2. Your CPA. After a few years of business, you will come to realize that a good CPA is one of the most valuable assets you can possibly have. I always tell my students to take their time selecting the right CPA, and make sure to find someone who wants to talk about the long-term growth and planning of your business.

Pro Tip: One of the most important considerations in choosing the right CPA is often referred to as "The Referral Rule" - put simply, make sure that you get a referral to a CPA by someone you know who is *successful* in business. You certainly wouldn't want to get a referral from someone who's been audited in the past few years! Obviously, this means one of the best places to start your CPA search is by asking established credit repair businesses whom they are using. Chances are, they'll be happy to refer you!

3. Your Name. The best advice I've ever gotten on choosing business names is also the shortest: "Simple and Strong!" The most important part of choosing a name, though, is making sure it's available. The Internet makes that incredibly easy. You want a name that sounds professional, evokes trust, and hopefully makes you stand out from the competition.

Pro Tip: It's better to be colorful than generic. Although many self-appointed experts will solemnly tell you to choose a name like "American National Credit Repair," something so bland might have the opposite effect you intended. Choosing a name that reflects your personality, your life experience, or something that identifies you as a local business are all preferable to a name that sounds like you're trying to hide something.

4. Your Website. Most of what you read on the subject of getting a website for your business will be hype. The two most important concepts for your entire online presence are **collection** and **conversion**. You want to have a clear path for potential leads to contact you, so your website is primarily there to help you collect their contact information so you can get back in touch with them, ASAP. This goes hand-in-hand with conversion, which is a measurement of how many visitors to your site wind up contacting you.

Pro tip: A lot of domain registry and hosting services will offer upgrades you don't need, but here's a few that you do. Automatic renewal is essential—it guarantees that you won't lose your domain to forgetfulness and simple mistakes. Another upgrade that's well worth the small cost is some sort of privacy option that makes it harder to gain information about your business from the domain listing. When people are snooping for data about you, make them contact you directly!

First, the Bad News...

With the passage of the Credit Repair Organizations Act in 1996, our industry had a new set of rules. One of the biggest changes was the provision that explicitly states, "A credit repair company cannot charge you until they have completed the promised services." This is unlike most other businesses you could start, but with the right planning, this is an easy hurdle to overcome.

The other main obstacle facing a new credit repair business is public perception. Many of your potential clients will associate the words "credit repair" with scams, frauds, and dire warning from federal agencies and state attorneys general!

Everyone in the business deals with skeptical customers. Thanks to years of credit repair industry propaganda, many Americans are wary of the term "credit repair" even if they don't fully understand why. This means that a big part of your job in securing clients will be education.

Ask any entrepreneur—the key to a successful business mindset is always perceiving problems as opportunities. So let's take a moment to flip both of these obstacles on their heads and turn them into advantages.

Now, not being able to get paid in advance is a simple inconvenience. There is a silver lining, though, and that's the additional confidence that your customers will feel knowing they don't have to pay for anything until they're gotten their money's worth. Since you can't change federal laws, this is the best perspective to have. There are several progressive models that allow you to receive payment quickly without violating the law, and as a buyer of this book, you get access to one of my Credit Industry Power Trainings that will discuss exactly how to legally get paid quickly in this industry.

Dealing with potential customers who are wary of credit repair can also work to your advantage. This is an opportunity to "wow" them with your quality information, clear presentation and upfront honesty. That might sound like a tall order, but that's probably because you're thinking you'll be alone in this.

That brings us to the good news—the really, really good news. You're not alone. I have spent many years now building a nationwide network that introduces new business owners like yourself to seasoned veterans and experienced mentors and gets you up to speed faster than you ever thought possible.

Your Support Network

For centuries now, Americans have loved reading inspirational stories about the self-made man. Looking back on my own path to success, though, there's no doubt in my mind that it was a group effort. My support network and my business mentors were absolutely critical to making me into an industry leader.

So when I help new credit repair business owners get started up, the very first thing I do is plug them into the incredible, nationwide support network we've been able to grow. Maintaining steady business and multiple income streams is always good business, but it's completely essential in credit repair. This is why I'm such a huge believer in the power of "mastermind" groups and powerful seminar events.

When you get frustrated, it's easy to feel alone—and it's critical to remember that you're not! Over the past decade, D.I.Y. entrepreneurs and one-person companies have been one of the few major growth sectors for the US economy. According to the US Census, "About three quarters of all US businesses have no payroll. Since 1997, non-employers have grown faster than employer firms."

One of my favorite parts of this job is our Credit Repair Boot Camp events. I try to top myself every time, assembling speakers like Joel Bauer, Jay Conrad Levinson, Jon Goldman, David Frees and Ron Quintero with even more interesting guests, like anonymous insiders from debt collection agencies, credit card companies, and even the credit bureaus themselves!

Our attendees always give us rave reviews, and they also say something that surprised me at first. Again and again, people tell us that the best part of the seminar was being able to network around the clock with fellow professionals from around the country! It is humbling that no matter how much firepower I assemble onstage, what I'm really doing is playing host to growing community of entrepreneurs who are helping each other survive and thrive.

Most industries have established methods for training and education, but—being a fairly new phenomenon—credit repair does not yet. One of my main professional goals is to change that. One of the biggest benefits of building this support network has been the boost it gives to the new entrepreneurs, and statistics show this is the group the needs help the most. It's no secret that most start-ups fail, and building a solid foundation takes time.

Collecting customer testimonials is a slow process when it takes many months to get conclusive results. It's great to talk about word-of-mouth marketing, but putting it into practice can be like *Mission Impossible* for a new business searching for their first few clients. During these early months, credit repair business owners need to be building other revenue streams and learning as much as they can about the industry.

There are several states that make it harder than usual to start a credit repair business (South Carolina and Georgia both come to mind) but yet, at any Boot Camp event you will find dozens of successful operators in the audience with you. We've learned how to make it happen in even the most hostile business environments. The collective intelligence of the Boot Camps is amazing. No matter what kind of obstacles you're facing, someone has been there before—and has beaten the odds. Best of all, they will be happy to teach you how it's done.

Another important benefit that our support network provides is giving us all a platform to set the record straight and correct internet rumors, false information, and the latest "scam of the week." To this day, people will still repeat poison lies about "wiping out bad credit" or "starting over with a new credit file"—when in fact, these claims and techniques will only make your situation worse!

We've made incredible progress in the last few years in presenting a unified front against this kind of disinformation and unethical "business." We have made tremendous progress turning our reputation around and are working towards making the credit repair industry known for what it truly stands for!

Networking Outside the Industry

Here's another win-win strategy that we teach at the Boot Camps. It's important to know other credit repair business owners from coast to coast, but it's equally important to know a wide variety of local professionals from other industries. Your clients will appreciate referral information for real estate agents, attorneys, the local Chamber of Commerce, any relevant state and federal agencies, even local banks! Sharing your Rolodex is an easy and mutually beneficial way to add value for your clients.

This really starts to pay off after you've started referring people to these professionals, because then they'll start to return the favor. Success is an ecosystem. As long as you're focused on providing service to your community, you'll reap the rewards of being a good corporate citizen!

The best part is that those aren't the only rewards to be gained—not by a long shot.

Teach to Learn

When I was a kid, I always did my homework. In the same spirit, I've put countless thousands of hours into researching the facts I'm presenting here, and the insights I've built into the DisputeSuite system. Looking back, though, I think that nothing has made me sharper than answering people's questions in public. Doing seminars and actively trying to teach this material is the best business move I ever made. It was incredible motivation to learn this entire industry like the back of my hand.

Starting out, I would get stumped. Often. I'll tell you what, though: people don't react like you might think. When you honestly tell them you don't know, nobody really holds it against you. This is the same industry that stumped a lawyer from the FTC, after all!

As I got more comfortable speaking to groups, I also found I had many more answers for people. Although there are millions of potential clients for your credit repair business, the bigger picture is millions more Americans who just need some honest information to help them make more informed decisions. Just by clearing up the common credit myths, you can save people in your audience from making expensive mistakes!

This is why education is the best form of business: you generate leads and more importantly, you have a positive effect on the larger community. As I always tell my students, "Go forth and help people!"

Clear Communication is Good Business

When you're starting out in business, it's normal to be nervous about your first customers. A great deal of work goes into that simple interaction. You need to calculate carefully to set your prices, you need to research the right system for getting the job done, and you need your documentation and presentation to be fully compliant with federal code. This sounds very complicated, but I do have some good news. In practice, it's very simple: A good relationship comes naturally when you put all your cards on the table.

The best way to prepare is just to imagine yourself in the customer's position. How often should they expect to hear from you? What kind of results should they expect from you? Exactly how long is a normal waiting period?

Here's more good news: you don't need to re-invent the wheel here, either. Not only is there an existing document that answers most of these questions, but it's legally mandatory that you provide potential clients with a copy before they sign any kind of contract. The full name is "Consumer Credit File Rights Under State and Federal Law."

I believe this is an excellent regulation, because it's a simple and upfront test of a credit repair agent's honesty and professionalism. Make sure consumers know their rights! Besides, over-promising will only lead to headaches and refunds—and if you're looking to go out of business fast, that's a great way to do it. This is a line of work where a "fast" resolution is around four months, so you want to be sure your client knows this is first and foremost a waiting game.

Now, here's a question that comes up a lot in Boot Camps. When I advocate laying all your cards on the table and educating potential clients *way* above and beyond what Federal regulations demand, I will always see a few skeptical faces in the crowd. Sure enough, one of them will raise their hand and ask me: "If we tell our customers how to do all of this themselves, how are we going to get any business?"

Well, that sounds like a fair question until you really think about it. After all, you probably know how to mow your lawn and maintain your front yard, yet millions and millions of US households will still happily hire someone else to do the work. Or consider H&R Block, who offer such a complete educational package that their customers could surely learn all the material and file their taxes themselves—but they don't. Time is the main consideration here, because we don't live in a world where we can learn or do everything.

When you're clear about what you're doing and upfront about being paid what you're worth, you'll find most potential clients you interact with will become paying customers. So it's very much worth it to make sure your customers know the formula and the process. There is no secret sauce in the credit repair industry.

There is a huge untapped market, though. One of the reasons that our Boot Camp events are such a huge boost for new business operators is the best possible problem an industry could have: an overflow of demand. It's easy to pass on leads because most established credit repair companies are simply overwhelmed by inquiries. This is the biggest reason I'm encouraging you to consider getting into this business. I know there's massive demand out there because I'm seeing it day after day, month after month...and the fact is, we *need* to bring in more people to cope with this tsunami.

I want to see people getting involved for the right reasons, though. When people try to feed you "Make Money in Your Sleep!" ad copy, you're right to be suspicious. Credit repair is a business, just like a grocery store or a factory, and there is plenty of work. It's also a lucrative opportunity for honest, ethical people to provide a service that will literally change the lives of struggling Americans. So let's take a look at the moral guidelines that will help keep you grounded—not to mention legally protected!

Some Guiding Principles

Think carefully about every claim you make. It's important to put this kind of attention into all of the copy associated with your business including your advertising, your website, your pamphlets and e-books, even your social networking presences. When you're brainstorming promotion ideas, or thinking up slogans and positioning statements, you don't always second-guess yourself. When it comes time to actually publish your work, though, go over it with a magnifying glass.

Ask your clients which items they want disputed. When you go over their reports with them, you will sometimes find completely accurate records and it's your obligation to tell them that, every time. Be polite but firm with customers who want you to misrepresent the facts and dispute accurate information. The bigger picture is your personal reputation. You will learn how to get inaccurate, outdated and unverifiable information removed from a consumer's credit report without violating the law.

Prepare yourself in advance for an investigation or audit of your business. This is advice I have been giving for years, and I've had a lot of students come back and tell me they wished they'd applied this back when I first told it to them. Believe me, you want to be ready. There are advantages that go way beyond merely covering your proverbial butt. By auditing yourself, you will find all kinds of hidden problems and wasteful spending, too. Your CPA and your bottom line will both agree that this kind of research is incredibly valuable.

Here's a real-world example of going further than compliance: keep a log of all the potential clients and leads that you turned down because you couldn't ethically help them. You don't need a detailed file, but you do need their names, contact information, and the reason you wouldn't enroll them into your credit repair program. If you're ever dealing with regulators, a document like this will be worth its weight in gold.

When you're in the credit repair business, you will quickly come to find that one office appliance suddenly becomes more valuable than you ever realized. That tool is the paper shredder. Setting up your business is a very straightforward process, and achieving success is just a matter of discipline. The discipline of strict privacy guidelines is completely essential. With a powerful software management system, most of the burden of compliance will become automatic. However, one thing that no subcontractor can do for you is handle documents correctly.

Many of businessmen and women who attend our Credit Repair Boot Camp events got into this line of work because they themselves have been victims of identity theft. They have learned firsthand what a long-term waking nightmare getting it can be to get these crimes resolved. You can bet they're taking their own privacy policies *very* seriously! You need to digitize and secure sensitive documents, and you need to regularly and thoroughly destroy all paper copies.

I always recommend having a careful disposal ritual, because this is one more way to go above and beyond mere compliance. Make sure to mix around and shake up shreddings, and don't throw out bags of shreddings along with your regular office trash. I know credit repair owner / operators who will drive document bags to the county landfill to be incinerated in front of them, or use special locked dumpsters and arrange a pickup with specialist contractors who come with trucks that chemically destroy the documents onsite. I also know a few serial entrepreneurs who got so dedicated to the science of document disposal and dealing with sensitive trash that they've even started side businesses providing that service locally.

The other half of this equation is digital security. One of the most common trends we've been seeing lately is larger credit repair operators using biometric ID systems to enter their workplace. Needless to say, this is an expensive option that you wouldn't need until you were dealing with some serious archives. For new businesses, though, a regular backup routine is mandatory. Your business literally is your data in this line of work, and you should protect that religiously.

Another common mistake that first-timers will make is sending sensitive documents over unsecured email. This is a *huge* error and if you got caught by federal or state regulators doing it, you would be liable for fines up to $10,000 *per page*. When you're just getting started, that means a single instance of this basic fumble could end your career! The most common solution is to use password protected PDFs for all sensitive communication. In fact, most of the established professionals will tell you to just go all the way and make *all* your communication and forwarded documents secured by strong passwords. "Better safe than sorry" takes on a whole new meaning when "sorry" amounts to five-figure fines.

Once you've gotten all this established, test your system. Go ahead and start adding in dummy clients like "John Sample" and checking, every step of the way, to be sure that your business is working at the nuts and bolts level. Don't get discouraged when tests reveal problems—be grateful. That's what testing is for, and there's nothing worse than discovering a problem when a paying customer points it out to you.

Speaking of paying customers, let's address them next. Now that you understand the steps behind setting up your own credit repair business, we're going to take a look at how to deal with customers and what your daily routine will look like once you get started.

Anatomy of a Contract

Most of the contracts I've seen in this business are five to seven pages long and very straightforward. You want to document your company's name, address and contact information and establish the length of the agreement upfront. Most standard contracts are month to month.

It is very important to clearly state the service you'll be providing in detail. Not only do you explain the results your client can expect, you should also list the specific actions you will perform on their behalf, and the cost for each. The customer will appreciate having a playbook to understand the process and they will have a "bill of goods" laying out precisely what they're paying for.

One aspect of contract language that all too often gets overlooked is privacy. We've already discussed the importance of a strict privacy process, so make sure you're advertising it. After all, during the course of your work you'll be entrusted with sensitive documents. Your customers definitely have the right to know exactly how those documents will be handled and secured.

Finally, the cancellation clause is a key part of staying compliant. You've got to spell out at least a three-day cancellation period to let your client change their mind—it's federal law and it's not optional. This must be displayed on three areas of your contract, but I suggest putting it on every page to be overly compliant. I often advise my student to beef up this period to at least five days. Remember: any client who would change their mind after the fact is not "losing money" so much as gaining peace of mind. They would have only been a complicated headache, and you're both better off parting ways early.

As you can see, the key to a successful credit repair business is proper setup. When you stick to the repeatable recipe we're outlining here, quality service, good relationships and customer satisfaction are built into the system. You only want to take clients you can legally help and reliably get results for. You want to be sure those clients have clear expectations on what services you will provide for them and what they're getting charged for. All that's left at this point is doing the work, and that's where DisputeSuite comes in.

Success by Design

The biggest advantage of a software management system like DisputeSuite is that it makes careful compliance completely automatic. There are a lot of online sources that will tell you that paperwork is a major challenge for a credit repair business. Apparently those authors are still doing business in the 1990s. With DisputeSuite, my team spent three years working closely with the most motivated and innovative professionals in the business. We worked alongside them, gave them the tools they needed, and constantly improved our software until we honed it into the powerful tool it is today.

Clearly, I'm biased and proud of my work. The fact is, though, even if you don't opt to use DisputeSuite and choose a more expensive, less powerful system, you absolutely must have some kind of management software. The alternative is insane. In this day and age, nobody should run a credit repair business out of a file cabinet. You will be only creating more work, more risks and more headaches for yourself.

The DisputeSuite system lets you manage all of your customers through an intuitive control panel—it's as simple as an email inbox. We've created tools for managing credit reports and automatically generating dispute letters from your client's file. We've provided a massive library of letter templates and a flexible editor so you can customize whatever you need. You can also manage employees, lead generation and sales activity, and all of this is done through the same easy interface.

Imagine replicating that with an analog system and you can see what I mean by "insane." DisputeSuite is proven to consistently save time and reduce risk. It's a tool that won't even let you make mistakes, and that's the most valuable employee you could ask for!

The Big Picture

The case for starting a credit repair business is beautifully simple. All in all, it's just a three-part formula: huge demand, reliable results and low cost of entry. Let's take a closer look at each of those.

Huge demand: There are millions and millions of Americans who are being punished for mistakes they have nothing to do with. They are victims of random and completely preventable errors.

Reliable results: There are clear, simple steps for disputing and correcting those errors, making sure they're removed, and improving your client's credit rating in the process.

Low cost of entry: Through years of Credit Repair Boot Camp events, I've seen some truly amazing success stories, and most of them started with a little bit of money and a lot of hard work.

When I introduced the DisputeSuite, it was a huge disruption to the credit repair industry, because I was providing a vastly superior product for thousands less than the existing competition. I opted for a low price point because it was simply the right thing to do. I knew it was time to democratize credit repair to transform it from a small, secretive fraternity to a thriving, modern industry. The runaway success and growth of the Credit Repair Boot Camp events has been proving me right ever since.

Go Forth and Help Somebody!

Even if you don't want to get started in the credit repair business, I'm still very grateful for your time and I hope this book was worth it. I'm sure you'll agree that the information I've laid out in this exposé is important to anyone in America with a job and a bank account.

So in closing this chapter, I'd like to ask you one favor: please pass this information along. Whether it's forwarding this exact report or just telling people about some of the facts you've learned here, you absolutely *can* make a difference by helping the people around you get educated about what a credit report really means, the true nature of the credit ratings agencies, and the shocking lack of government oversight of their industry.

The situation is ugly but it's far from hopeless. As the public learns more about this sad state of affairs, they will create the pressure needed to finally change things. I didn't write this to point fingers because I'm not interested in blame, I'm interested in solutions. Once we perceive the problem, we can get started on fixing it.

The American people deserve better.

Chapter 11 - Update: The New Final Frontier

In Chapter 5 I discussed what, at the time of writing, I thought was the "final frontier" for the greedy, unethical misbehavior of the credit bureaus... namely, the monetization of consumers with good credit through fear-mongering over "ID Theft" and swooping in with quasi-effective credit monitoring services to give consumers a false sense of security that they'd be willing to pay top dollar for.

The problem, of course, is that consumers can get better protection for less money by way of a "credit freeze". The services offered by the credit bureaus to "protect" you from identity theft are not much more than a facade. They are made to look like one thing—the credit bureaus doing their part to help the consumer—but in reality they are something totally different... i.e. the credit bureaus profiting further from their own inaccurate data (by design) through the use of fear.

Today I can tell you (unfortunately) that there's a new final frontier that you and I should be concerned with. The credit bureaus have gone "back to the drawing board" in monetizing the bad credit crowd, and have come out with what is perhaps the most brazen, unethical slap in the face that the credit system has ever seen.

Before I tell you what the new service is, let me give you a little illustration to put it in perspective.

> *Imagine for a moment that a person named Bob had a business that specialized in building engines. Let's just say, for the sake of illustration, that this was the only place in the country to buy an engine of any kind. Anyone who needed an engine had to get it from Bob's engine service. You could say that Bob had a monopoly... and he was loving it.*
>
> *But Bob's engine business needed more customers and more money, which meant more people had to buy more engines. So Bob did something most of us would consider pretty unethical. He intentionally designed his engines so that they would fail, and do so frequently. This way people would have to buy more and more engines.*
>
> *But then companies started popping up all over that specialized in fixing engines. That was a problem for Bob. So Bob worked with lawmakers to get laws passed to make it as difficult as possible for other companies to make money fixing the engines that Bob designed. Then he changed his designs to make fixing them even more difficult yet.*
>
> *Finally, once Bob had put shackles on the feet of every engine-repair shop in the country and locked consumers into buying and re-buying his shoddy poor quality engines, Bob once again acted in a way that most of us would probably consider quite unethical. Bob opened up his own engine repair shop so that he could further capitalize on the failure of his engines. He was in the perfect position: not only could he design the engines to fail, but he could become the "only game in town" when it came to fixing them.*

Now maybe you already know where I'm headed with this but I've got to say it anyways. The credit bureaus—the ones who have been profiting from inaccurate data and thwarting the efforts of consumers and credit repair companies to fix that inaccurate data for years—have entered a new area of business:

The CREDIT REPAIR (AND ADVICE) Business.

Yes, you read that right. The credit bureaus have found a NEW way to monetize their inaccurate data and the "bad credit crowd", and to further monetize the credit repair and credit dispute processes: They are getting into the credit repair business!

Experian, in a move that is unprecedented in the history of our modern credit system, has started a credit repair/advice service that meets the definition of a "Credit Repair Organization" as defined by the CROA and is therefore governed by the Credit Repair Organizations Act.

This unprecedented move probably looked pretty boring to the casual passerby, but don't underestimate it. It's an important move that could affect the credit industry in many ways for years to come.

Experian's new service goes something like this:

The consumer pays $29.95 to see their credit reports, review their non-fico score, and ask questions from a generic selection of categories with an Experian agent on the phone for about 20 minutes.

According to their website, here's what you get when you sign up for the service:

- Approximately 20 minutes of phone time with a "credit educator" agent.
- A walkthrough of what's on your credit report.
- Your credit score (NON-FICO score) and regional/state/national benchmark scores for comparison.
- An explanation of what contributes to your current credit score
- And last by not least... "Insight for future decisions in credit management."[2]

In other words, the service Experian offers doesn't do anything more than any qualified credit repair professional can do. In fact, it does a lot LESS and it does it for a lot MORE money.

At the cost of $29.95 for 20 minutes of time, Experian is charging the equivalent of $90 per hour to give consumers advice on improving and managing their credit.

Take a look at what the company press release said about the launch of this service...

"The economic recession has significantly changed consumer awareness and attitudes toward

---

[2] Source: www.Experian.com

credit and we found that consumers were asking Experian for assistance in taking a more active role in understanding their credit. The Credit Educator program is our response to this consumer request and provides a dedicated one-on-one focus on credit education to increase dialogue and provide personalized tips for maintaining a healthy credit profile,"[3]

What Experian is really saying here is simple: "The trouble with the economy has resulted in some people struggling with their credit and wanting to improve the situation, and we're ready to cash in on it!"

Experian is selling advice... *very expensive* advice. <u>And I'm not even convinced that it's good advice, either</u>. In an article on USNews.com one author who tested the service for free was told by the agent that he had "too many inquiries". How many was too many? ONE! [4]

So Experian has a Credit Repair Organization that gives consumers credit advice, and they do it without actually helping anyone to fix anything. Leave it to the credit bureaus to start a "Credit Repair Organization" as defined by the CROA that doesn't actually fix a thing.

It's like Bob's engine repair for Bob's shoddy engines, with no repairs actually taking place! (At least you get to ask questions about your broken engine, right?)

All kidding aside, this step is an important one that you and I need to pay attention to. The credit bureaus entering the credit repair business is the next stage in the ongoing saga of the "Credit Bureaus Suck" story. It is yet another way for the credit bureaus to profit from bad credit, from inaccurate data, and from their own epic failures to properly protect consumer data.

And it's only just begun...

---

[3] Source: http://www.prnewswire.com
[4] Source: http://money.usnews.com

Chapter 12 - Credit Bureaus Suck: The Government Takes Notice

In 2010, the Consumer Finance Protection Bureau (or CFPB) was created, primarily in response to the failures of the financial industry in the several years prior. The CFPB exists for consumer protection. It is a government agency that now holds most of the consumer protection authority in the financial markets. The CFPB—according to their website—will write rules, clarify regulations, "curb" unfair and abusive practices, promote financial education, enforce laws, and conduct research related to their tasks.

The creation of the CFPB may be good for the credit system and the credit repair industry in the long run. In this chapter I'll explain why.

The 2012 CFPB Report

A report released by the CFPB in December of 2012 focused on the credit bureaus and their operations in the credit system, and highlighted many failings that myself and others have been pointing out for years. Here are a few highlights from the 2012 CFPB Report on the credit bureaus:

- The CFPB noted that Social Security Numbers are not included (or required) for the majority of credit reporting activities. In one example provided, it was estimated that only 3% of public records submitted to the credit bureaus through LexisNexis contain Social Security Numbers. The CFPB acknowledges that the variations in data requirements and the data collected and submitted by furnishers are factors that complicate credit reporting and therefore contribute to some of the problems experienced in the industry.

- According to the CFPB report, the quality control performed on incoming data is limited mainly to logical comparisons and algorithms to detect when the incoming data doesn't make any sense at all. There is no effort made to verify the actual accuracy of the data itself.

- The credit bureaus do not immediately accept all data submitted. A lot of data is initially rejected due to not passing their automated quality control checks. An interesting note is that submissions from collection agencies have higher rejection rates than submissions for credit card trade lines.

- The credit bureaus get most or all of their public record data through LexisNexis Risk Data Retrieval Services LLC ("LexisNexis" for short). All bankruptcy records originate from Pacer, along with 30% of the records on judgments. Most of the other data is obtained through a network of contractors who visit the courthouses and physically input the data into LexisNexis databases.

- The over 50% of furnisher-submitted data comes from the top 1% of furnishers. In other words, a few big furnishers supply the credit bureaus with most of their payment and account data.

- The highest dispute rates relative to the number of accounts submitted occur for the smallest furnishers. The smaller the furnisher is, the more dispute-prone the accounts are.

- The CFPB states correctly that a key part of the credit reporting process—and therefore an area of concern—is the *data matching process* used by the credit bureaus. The task of matching the right data to the right consumer is of great importance to the accuracy of credit reports.

- Factors cited that complicate the matching process included the inconsistencies among furnishers in reporting practices and the information collected, furnisher data quality practices, the fact that many consumers have similar names and change names in their lifetime (such as when a person gets married), and the lack of "key identifiers" such as Social Security Numbers.

- The CFPB also talked about the "partial matches" that the credit bureau matching algorithms do, stating that: "In some cases, matching algorithms will assign the trade line to a file that, according to the algorithm, represents the best match even when all of the identifiers do not match up perfectly, or when only a limited number of identifiers are contained within the trade line."

- The CFPB discussed e-OSCAR, and the lack of a mechanism to forward documentation (i.e. "all relevant information") through the e-OSCAR System.

Why The CFPB May Be Good For The Industry

For years there has been a lot of finger pointing in the credit and credit repair industries. Consumer advocates (including myself) have repeatedly pointed out the flaws and errors with the credit reporting system, and the numerous injustices that consumers have experienced at the hands of the credit bureaus, furnishers, and collectors. The CFPB may be a step in the right direction, if for no other reason than the facts that:

A. The agency was created with enough authority to ACT, and

B. The agency has committed itself to taking a close look at the credit reporting industry and its effect on consumers.

It is my belief that it is quite impossible for someone to do point "B" without getting concerned and/or passionate about the mistreatment of consumers in the credit system. It could therefore be quite positive, in the long run, that finally the entity that is taking on "point B" has a substantial amount of authority to act on their findings.

Considering that the CFPB has "point A" (i.e. authority to act), it can be nothing but positive that they are making the examination of the credit bureaus and their practices a top priority.

The fact that the agency created to protect consumers in the financial markets has decided to make the examination of the credit bureaus and their practices a top priority is, in itself, quite telling. It tells us that not only do the *credit bureaus suck*, but that the government has noticed that the credit bureaus suck, and wants to do something about it.

The CFPB appears to have put two and two together when it comes to credit reporting. It is the credit bureaus that design the systems and write the policies that facilitate the entire credit reporting process. If there are problems with the process, it is logical to conclude that the credit bureaus themselves should be the starting point for an investigation.

What It Means For Credit Repair

Contrary to what some may believe, improvements in the accuracy of data and the systems for data reporting and disputes would all be positive developments for the banks, the credit card companies, AND for the credit repair industry.

Even in a system that is not so heavily geared against consumers, errors will still happen—consumers will still need help with their credit—there will still be work to do. If the system improves, then (in theory) many of the more time consuming and difficult-to-correct situations should be reduced in both frequency and severity. If the system improves, then legitimate factual disputes ought to become even more effective for correcting errors.

If the system improves, the sub-prime market for credit will still exist—but it will be a more marketable and profitable sub-prime market. There will be less credit score damage that results from the system itself, and this will create positive opportunities for consumers, banks, credit card companies, and credit repair companies. For people involved in credit repair, the creation of the CFPB may eventually translate into things like:

- More effective disputes
- More responsive credit bureaus, furnishers, and collectors
- Fewer ancillary errors and issues, more ability to focus on the real problems
- A broader and healthier sub-prime market, with more consumers able to take advantage of the new and better credit products that are likely to become available to them.

It Starts and Ends With the Credit Bureaus

As of this writing, the credit bureaus *still suck*. The government has noticed, though, and this could eventually mean good things for the industry. The real question is: *now that the government has noticed, what exactly are they going to do about it?* We can hope that good will come from the creation of the CFPB and its examination of the credit bureaus and the credit reporting industry. Only time will tell what the reality will be.

About the Author

Michael Citron has revolutionized the credit repair industry by creating the state-of-the-art software system DisputeSuite.com, designed for credit repair business owners. The software provides all of the tools needed to successfully start, manage, and grow successful credit repair companies. As the leader in software for the credit repair industry worldwide, DisputeSuite has adapted its technology to be used around the globe. DisputeSuite's web-based credit repair software application is used on four continents, in every state in the US, Puerto Rico, Guam and the US Virgin Islands.

In-depth, advanced credit repair training is available through Credit Biz in a Box—a groundbreaking training course for those in the credit repair industry. Mike describes it as "the ultimate solution for anyone in the credit repair business, whether starting out or a veteran, with over 5,000 pages of easy-to-digest information is packed with knowledge not available elsewhere."

Since founding the industry's first successful multi-day training conference at CreditBootCamp.com, Mike has been gaining momentum in uniting other credit industry leaders in a non-profit association, the National Association of Responsible Credit Repair Advisors. Their goal is to help educate the consumer and to fight the battles with the credit bureaus. He is a true consumer advocate and a champion of the legal processes that benefit the consumer. His work is enabling the credit repair companies to gain greater credibility, which in turn makes them more effective when negotiating with the credit bureaus on behalf of the consumer.

Mike has made it his mission to educate the public and empower them to rebuild their credit. His organizations are devoted to providing the tools and resources necessary to credit repair companies to help consumers. His belief is that credit repair companies have been burdened with inefficient, overpriced technology and education for too long, and he has made it his mission to provide cost-effective training and software solutions for all members of the credit repair industry.

Made in the USA
Middletown, DE
10 April 2021